THE POCKET GUIDE TO

Camping

THE POCKET GUIDE TO

Camping

LINDA WHITE
& KATHERINE L. WHITE

Illustrations by Remie Geoffroi

GIBBS SMITH
TO ENRICH AND INSPIRE HUMANKIND

Manufactured in Altona, Manitoba, Canada in April 2011 by Friesen

First Edition
15 14 13 12 11   5 4 3

NOTE: Some of the activities suggested in this book require adult assistance and supervision. Activities associated with camping and the outdoors carry inherent risks. The publisher and authors assume no responsibility for any damages or injuries incurred while performing any of the activities in this book.

Published by
Gibbs Smith
P.O. Box 667
Layton, Utah 84041

1.800.835.4993 orders
www.gibbs-smith.com

Designed by Michel Vrana
Gibbs Smith books are printed on either recycled, 100% post-consumer waste, FSC-certified papers or on paper produced from sustainable PEFC-certified forest/controlled wood source. Learn more at www.pefc.org.

Library of Congress Cataloging-in-Publication Data
White, Linda, 1948-
  Pocket guide to camping / Linda White & Katherine L. White ; illustrations by Remie Geoffroi. — 1st ed.
    p. cm.
  ISBN 978-1-4236-2058-7
  1. Camping—Handbooks, manuals, etc. I. White, Katherine L. II. Title.
  GV191.7.W58 2011
  796.54—dc22

                                    2010052576

CONTENTS

★★★

CHAPTER ONE

Packing

AND

PREPARING

What are you going to do this weekend? Watch TV, play video games, clean your room? Would you rather sing songs around a blazing campfire, roast marshmallows on a stick until they are gooey, and sleep in a sack under the stars? Then you should go camping!

GETTING STARTED

Getting started in the world of camping can be confusing. Outdoor shops offer oodles of choices in equipment and gadgets. Fortunately, you don't have to buy everything you see there. Much of what you need you probably already have. Add a few basics—mainly a tent and a good sleeping bag—learn a few camp skills, and you'll be ready to head for the woods.

The best camping trips are well-planned ones. It's no fun to be miles from any town, have the wood laid for your campfire, and your hot dogs on a stick, only to find out you've forgotten to bring matches. There'll be a cold and hungry night ahead!

This book will help you organize a great camping trip. You'll learn what to look for when choosing camp equipment; what food, clothes, and tools to pack; how to choose and set up a camp home; and some games, songs, and crafts to keep you entertained while you're living in the wild.

Having an adult camp with you is a must. You'll be going places you haven't been before, doing new things, and using unfamiliar tools. You'll want an adult to help you purchase gear, set up camp, know when it's safe to build a campfire, and many other things. Besides, it's always more fun to do things together.

When you see this symbol, the use of something sharp, such as a knife, ax, or camp saw, is required.

This symbol alerts you to a burn hazard. Make sure to ask an adult for help when doing these tasks.

Can you smell the wood smoke? Are you ready to hear the night music of the out-of-doors? Let's go camping!

WHERE TO GO

Start out by picking your favorite camping site. Do you want to go to the woods or the beach? To the mountains or the desert? Do you want to go to a favorite family campsite that you return to year after year? Or try someplace new? Do you want to drive a long way by car or plan a short trip?

Have an adult help you decide where a good place to camp will be. Then research the time of year, how long it takes to get there, how many campsites are available, whether the campsite requires reservations, maps for the best route, and so on. You'll want to plan your trip in advance so you know where you're going and what you'll need.

CAUTION: Don't throw your gear in the car, ride to your destination, and think you'll find the perfect camping spot on the banks of the swimming hole. You may end up with your tent pitched ten feet

from the highway, or not get a campsite at all. Remember the early camp bird gets a campsite!

Many campgrounds now allow campers to make reservations. Some require reservations or permits that you must apply for well in advance of your trip. A guide to campgrounds (available at bookstores and libraries) will give you the information you need and provide a phone number to call with questions. There is also often a lot of good information about local campsites on the Internet.

WHERE YOU'LL SLEEP

You'll miss a real treat if you don't sleep out sometimes where you can count the stars. But since the weather can change suddenly, a tent—your portable home—is desirable for most camping trips. It'll keep the rain out of your face and the mosquitoes out of your ears. It'll also give you a private place to change clothes.

Backpacking tents, used by campers hiking deep into the backcountry, hold one or two campers in close quarters. These tents may weigh as little as five or six pounds. Good ones can cost several hundred dollars.

Dome tents, shaped like a turtle shell, can be a good choice for a small family or a few friends. They are easy to set up, sturdy, and come in a range of prices (and qualities). But watch out when the tag says the tent sleeps three—that may not include room for even the next day's clothes!

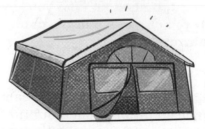

Larger, cabin-style tents, made like a cloth building with walls and a roof, are great choices for big groups and when you're going on longer outings. The extra space and stand-up headroom really make a difference.

Many campers like campgrounds that are for tent campers only. That way they aren't kept awake by a loud recreational vehicle generator powering an even louder television. Most tent campers prefer watching stars, listening to animals, singing around the campfire, and telling stories for their evening entertainment.

Firewood gathering is not allowed in many campgrounds. Find out before you go, and, if needed, take your own or see if you can buy it at the camp headquarters.

PACKING

People new to camping, and even some longtime campers, usually take too much or too little on their wilderness adventures. The following lists will help you decide what to take on your camping trip. Some things are essential; others may not be, depending on the type of camping you are doing. If you're camping in a motor home, you won't need a tent. If you plan to burrow into a snow cave, leave the shorts at home. After you've made a few trips, make a list that suits your own kind of camping. Then you can refer back to it when preparing for your next outing.

Here's a sample packing list of things you might want to take.

For cooking

- ☐ Aluminum foil
- ☐ Resealable plastic bags
- ☐ Shovel
- ☐ Wire grill
- ☐ Can opener
- ☐ Pots, pans, or coffee cans
- ☐ Knife
- ☐ Pitcher or bucket
- ☐ Long-handled tongs
- ☐ Bucket of dirt/sand and turner

☐ Heat-proof spatula
☐ Oven mitts or wooden spoon
☐ Measuring cups and spoons
☐ Matches
☐ Portable kitchen timer or wristwatch

For cleanup

☐ Plastic grocery and trash bags
☐ Dishcloth
☐ Washtub
☐ Biodegradable soap

For eating

☐ Dishes (paper or reusable)
☐ Silverware (plastic or regular)
☐ Napkins
☐ Cups (paper, plastic, Styrofoam, or tin)
☐ Table cover
☐ Salt, pepper, ketchup, salsa, and other condiments

Miscellaneous

- ☐ Ice chest or insulated container with ice or ice packs
- ☐ Insect repellent
- ☐ First aid kit
- ☐ Sunscreen
- ☐ Flashlight
- ☐ Camera

First Aid Kit

- ☐ Bandages
- ☐ Aspirin or ibuprofen
- ☐ Calamine lotion
- ☐ Antibiotic cream or ointment
- ☐ Tweezers
- ☐ Scissors or nail clippers
- ☐ Moist towelettes
- ☐ Bandages
- ☐ Adhesive gauze
- ☐ Moleskin for blisters
- ☐ Plastic bag for rain protection
- ☐ Lip balm

MEAL PLANNING

Is there a camp store where you are going where you can purchase forgotten items? If not, pack carefully. Imagine getting to camp without the chocolate bars for your s'mores. Your trip could be ruined!

Once you know how long you'll be camping, plan the meals. Try the recipes in this book (chapter 4). You'll need breakfast, lunch, dinner, and snacks for each day in the woods.

There are no kitchens in the woods. You have to bring your own. But how do you know what to take, especially if you've never done much cooking in the kitchen at home? Don't panic. For short trips, you can cook your food over an open fire on a stick, and all you'll need in order to eat dinner is a cup, plate, and eating utensils. For longer trips, you'll want a variety of foods, so you'll need more equipment. Planning ahead will help things go smoothly.

The risk of forest fires is always present, and it is higher in the summertime. Some parks, counties, and states limit the kinds of fires you can have, and when and where you can have them. Most fire bans are for wood fires. If your area has a high fire danger, you might need to use gas or charcoal grills rather than having an open fire pit to cook your dinner. Plan ahead and have an adult help you find out what kinds of fires are okay in your area.

NOTE: Safety is your most important responsibility. An adult should be with you at all times when you are cooking or doing activities in this book.

COOKING SUPPLIES

Before going on a cookout, there are some things you need to make and gather.

Cooking sticks can be used to cook many kinds of campfire meals. The right kinds of sticks are not always available at campsites, so make your own reusable cooking stick. Instructions are on pages 208–10.

Oven mitts and **barbecue cooking tools** help protect your hands from the heat of the campfire. Oven mitts are thick, padded mittens. Use them when handling hot foods and equipment. Barbecue tools such as long-handled turners, tongs, and forks allow you to stand back from the fire to tend your food and keep you from getting too close to the flames. Also remember, when cooking always keep a bucket of water nearby. If sparks or flames land on your mitts or clothing, use your bucket of water to drench them immediately.

Aluminum foil is a valuable tool around the camp. You can cook meals in it, make cooking and serving containers, and wrap leftovers to take home. Heavy-duty foil works best, but three layers of regular-strength foil can also be used.

Most campsites have metal grates to cook on, but not all. Metal grates are hard to find in the forest or out on the range, so consider taking your own! A variety of inexpensive wire cooking grills are available at outdoor shops. If you buy a medium- or large-sized grill, you'll be able to cook more food at once. You can also use it to hold your food over the fire when your arm gets tired or you need to do something else.

PLASTIC TOTE BOXES

Plastic tote boxes, such as those sold as fishing tackle boxes and sewing kits, can be used to hold camp cooking gear. Put cooking utensils such as tongs, wooden spoons, and spatulas in the bottom. Small things (including matches, salt, pepper, and spices) can be kept in the top tray between the dividers. Get a tote box to use just for camp gear. Don't use the smelly one your brother takes fishing!

You probably have **measuring cups and spoons** at home, but if not, purchase a set of each. These sets usually contain cups to measure $\frac{1}{8}$, $\frac{1}{4}$, $\frac{1}{2}$, and 1 cup. They fit neatly inside each other, so they don't take up much room. Measuring spoon sets usually contain $\frac{1}{4}$, $\frac{1}{2}$, and 1 teaspoon, and 1 tablespoon measures. When you measure, fill the cup or spoon to the top and level off the ingredients with the back of a table knife.

Sealable plastic bags in pint, quart, $\frac{1}{2}$-gallon, and gallon sizes have many uses while camping. You can mix and season ingredients in them. You can also use them for storing leftovers and separating wet or dirty items, such as dirty silverware, wet bathing suits, or messy cleanup rags. Use the ones marked "freezer bags." They are heavier than the regular ones, which helps keep them from splitting while you are mixing or carrying foods.

A **first aid kit** should be on hand to treat cuts, burns, and insect bites. A kit might include bandages, antiseptic ointment, aspirin, and calamine lotion. Purchase a first aid kit from a drugstore or outdoor shop, or make your own.

If you are traveling a long distance to your campout, be especially careful to keep foods that need to be refrigerated cold until they are used. (The labels on most foods will tell you if they need to be refrigerated.) An insulated plastic storage chest with some ice packs will usually do the trick.

Some miscellaneous items to bring along that will be very helpful include the following:

- ☐ Spatulas
- ☐ Wire coat hangers
- ☐ Newspaper for starting fires
- ☐ Charcoal
- ☐ Nonstick cooking spray
- ☐ Shovel
- ☐ Flashlight
- ☐ Lantern

☐ Extra batteries
☐ Camera and film
☐ Plates
☐ Sunscreen
☐ Insect repellent
☐ Toilet paper

CLOTHING

Your regular old clothes are ideal for camping. Camp days often start and end with a cold temperature, with a warm period in the middle. That makes it hard to decide what to wear. Layering your clothes is the answer! Layering means wearing several pieces of light-weight clothing rather than one heavy piece. The air between the layers traps and holds your body heat, keeping you warm. As the day warms up, make like a banana and peel those layers! Add them back on as the day cools down.

Try these layers:

★ Underwear + T-shirt + long-sleeved shirt + sweatshirt + jacket
★ Shorts + jeans
★ Cap or sunhat and sunscreen
★ Long underwear + shirt + long-sleeved T-shirt + sweatshirt/wool sweater + vest + scarf + parka
★ Sweatpants + loose-fitting pants
★ Glove liners + waterproof gloves
★ Cotton socks + wool socks
★ Raincoat/poncho + waterproof pants + waterproof boots

A note about socks: Thick cotton socks keep your feet cool in hot weather and warm in cool weather. Thick woolly socks protect hiking feet from blisters. Wool socks stay warm even when wet, making them the best choice for cold weather. Socks can be layered, too!

A note about shoes: Rubber sport sandals are the best choice if you will be around water. Wear sneakers or hiking boots for hiking, and make sure you have something easy to slip into for the midnight trip to the outhouse.

Depending on the weather, you can sleep in these: fresh cotton-knit T-shirt and shorts, sweats, thermal underwear, or pajamas. Be sure you change into sleeping attire and a pair of dry socks before going to bed. If you sleep in the clothes you wore during the day, they will have moisture from your body in them and you will have a hard time staying warm during the night.

GEAR

The kind of camping you do, where you camp, and how long you stay determines what you take. Different campgrounds, whether perched beside shining seas, in tall grasses, or on mountaintops, offer different facilities. Some have showers and flush toilets, while in primitive campgrounds you'll have to dig a pit for a toilet. Check in the library, bookstore, or online to find what facilities each campground has before you go there.

The time of year you camp also changes the gear you take. Summer campers often strap bicycles on top of their cars before they head out. Winter campers build snow caves and snuggle in below the howling winds and deep snows. They leave the tent at home and pack extra warm clothes and sleeping bags. It's important to be prepared. Check the weather forecast for the place you're heading and plan and pack appropriately.

Now let's take a look at what gear you need.

- ☐ Tent
- ☐ Sleeping Bag
- ☐ Clothing
- ☐ Food and Cooking Gear
- ☐ First Aid Kit

Here are some important smaller things to take on your camping trip. Store them in waterproof containers (self-sealing plastic bags work fine) where they will stay dry. Keep them where you can find them.

- ☐ Maps
- ☐ Matches (store them in a small watertight container to keep dry)
- ☐ Flashlight with extra batteries
- ☐ Emergency candle (in case your flashlight gets lost or broken)
- ☐ Safety pins
- ☐ Needle and thread (for clothing and gear repair)
- ☐ Compass

- ☐ Emergency whistle (Keep in your pocket, or attached to a zipper, or on a cord around your neck. Use it only to call for help.)
- ☐ Nylon cord (to make a clothesline or hang food in trees out of reach of animals)
- ☐ Clothespins (to secure wet clothes and dishcloths on clothesline to dry)
- ☐ Trowel or small shovel (to dig a pit toilet and a food-scrap hole where there are no trash cans)
- ☐ Water jug

Use these only when an adult says it's okay:

- ☐ Pocketknife (Some pocketknives have tweezers, a screwdriver, pliers, and other handy tools in addition to several knife blades.)
- ☐ Backpacker's saw (for cutting wood when you have to)

PACKS

Now you've got your gear together, will you have to juggle it along the trail? Of course not! You'll carry all that paraphernalia in a pack. They come in several sizes and styles to suit different needs.

Are you going for an hour-long hike along the beach or a two-day winter hike in the mountains? The trappings you pack depend on where you are going and how long you'll be gone. In any case, remember: anything you take, you carry. So pack as little as possible, but don't forget the necessities. Make sure everything you take is lightweight. Your pack will be much lighter, and when you're camping or on the trail, you'll be glad it is!

Waist packs clip around your waist and have enough room for a few items only. Use one when taking a short hike.

Daypacks are carried on your back and are large enough to carry the needs of a full day.

Backpacks are a larger version of the daypack. Built on a metal framework, there's room in them to pack enough for trips that will last more than one day.

How many pounds should you carry in your pack? A growing kid shouldn't lug more than 20 percent of his or her body weight. To find out how much that is, divide your weight by five. Example: If you weigh sixty pounds, divide that by five. So your pack and everything in it shouldn't weigh more than twelve pounds. What's your limit?

If you are purchasing new equipment, tell the clerk at the outdoor shop what kind of camping and hiking you plan to do. She will be able to show you several pack models that are right for your needs. She'll explain their features and fit the pack to you.

Search for these features:

★ padded shoulder straps ★ padded back ★ reinforced stitching ★ smooth-working zippers covered with a flap ★ sturdy, waterproof, rip-resistant fabric ★ outside compartments ★ two-layered pack bottom ★ the right size for you ★ waist straps on day packs ★ waist and chest straps on backpacks ★ reflector strips ★

Ask the salesperson to load up the packs you are trying to decide between with a load similar in weight to what you'll carry on the trail. Try out each pack. Wear it around the store. See which feels best. Tell the clerk about any problems. Sometimes a simple strap adjustment will make a world of difference.

SNACKS

You're not likely to find a hamburger stand or take-out pizza at your campsite. In addition to packing meals for your outing, it's important to have snacks for hiking or to give you energy throughout the day. At the very least, take something to nibble on in case you aren't able to get back from a hike or prepare dinner as quickly as planned.

Here's a list of great grub for the trail and some recipes that will keep you searching for a shady spot to take a rest. Any of the following food items will pack well and satisfy your hunger.

ON-THE-GO SNACKS

- ☐ Dried fruits
- ☐ Nuts
- ☐ Hard-boiled eggs
- ☐ Sandwich foods such as peanut butter, cheese, and canned meats or fish
- ☐ Whole-grain breads
- ☐ Cookies
- ☐ Instant breakfast drinks
- ☐ Fruit juices
- ☐ Fresh fruits and vegetables

SNACK RECIPES

Peppermint Orange

WHAT YOU NEED:

1 orange (Valencia oranges work best)
1 peppermint stick

WHAT YOU DO:

1. Roll the orange on the picnic table to loosen the juice.

2. With a small knife, cut a cone-shaped hole in one end of the orange.

3. Put the candy stick in the hole.

4. Bite the end off the candy stick and suck on it as you would a straw. It may take a little while to get the juice started.

GORP (Good Old Raisins and Peanuts)

WHAT YOU NEED:

2 cups roasted peanuts
1/2 cup raisins
1 cup of any of these: chocolate candies, licorice bits, chocolate chips, nuts, seeds, dried fruit, pretzels, dry cereal

WHAT YOU DO:

1. Pour ingredients into a half-gallon sealable plastic bag and shake to mix.

2. Pack in small pocket-sized bags to take along on the trail.

Peanut Butter Logs

WHAT YOU NEED:

1/2 cup peanut butter
1/2 cup dry milk powder
1/4 cup honey
1 tablespoon cocoa powder
1/4 cup chopped nuts
1/4 cup raisins
1/4 cup coconut (optional)

WHAT YOU DO:

1. Dump all ingredients into a one-quart sealable plastic bag.

2. Squeeze bag gently until all ingredients are mixed.

3. Divide mixture into eight equal pieces.

4. Roll each piece into a log. Wrap each log in plastic wrap.

Trail Mix

WHAT YOU NEED:

¼ cup butter
1 tablespoon Worcestershire sauce
¾ teaspoon salt
½ teaspoon garlic powder
¼ teaspoon onion powder
6 cups multigrain Chex cereal
1 cup peanuts or mixed nuts
1 cup small pretzels
1 cup bite-sized bagel chips

WHAT YOU DO:

1. Heat oven to 250 degrees F.

2. Melt butter in a baking pan in the oven.

3. Stir in all seasonings.

4. Stir in all dry ingredients. Mix until all ingredients are evenly coated.

5. Bake 45 minutes, stirring every 15 minutes.

6. Spread on paper towels to cool.

7. Divide mixture into 1-cup servings and put in sealable plastic bags.

OTHER RESOURCES

As you spend more and more time camping and hiking, your list of questions will grow. How was this land formed? How did the mountains get so high? Why is the lake so deep here? What is the altitude? How does that affect what grows here? What birds live here? Do they live here all year long or are they seasonal? Do the trees here lose their leaves in the winter or are they evergreen?

Trail and nature guides about your area offer the most specific information. These are available in bookstores; nature centers; and recreation, park, and forest-service offices. You can also research online before you go and when you get home.

Encyclopedias offer a wealth of information on most general subjects you can think of. Look up information on deer, cedar trees, or rocks.

Libraries have hundreds of books to keep you reading about all the trail subjects that stir your interest. Look in the nonfiction section of your library. If you have questions or need help finding something, an adult or librarian will be happy to help you.

Here are some other places to check out:

- ☐ National Audubon Society
- ☐ Boy Scouts of America
- ☐ Girl Scouts of the USA
- ☐ Campfire Boys and Girls
- ☐ American Red Cross
- ☐ Eddie Bauer
- ☐ Eastern Mountain Sports
- ☐ L. L. Bean
- ☐ Gibbs Smith, Publisher

WHAT TO PACK

Clothes:

....

....

....

....

....

Toiletries:

....

....

....

....

....

Entertainment:

....

....

....

....

....

SHOPPING LIST

CHAPTER TWO

Pitching

CAMP

If you arrive at the campground and there is just one campsite left, grab it. If you have a choice, though, think about these things when deciding which place to take. The ideal campsite

★ is roomy enough for sleeping, cooking, sitting, and cleanup areas;

★ is screened from neighboring campsites by trees and bushes;

★ has a level spot free of rocks and sticks that is large enough for your tent;

★ is sunny in the morning and shady in the afternoon;

★ is near the restroom, but not so close that the smell or traffic are problems;

★ is not in a low spot, which can collect moisture, have bugs, and get puddles when it rains.

After you have checked out the camp and dipped your feet in the stream, the first thing you will do is set up your camp home. Camp, like everything else, is better with a little organization.

SETTING UP THE COOKING AREA

Cooking and cleanup won't seem like such a chore if you store everything you need near the picnic table and fire ring. The picnic table will serve as your food center. If you are using a camp stove, put it at one end of the table, making sure it is level. The ice chest can be placed on the bench beside it. While preparing the meal, your utensil caddy can be on the table so you can easily reach a knife for chopping and a spoon for mixing.

While your meal is cooking, change the picnic table from food center to dinner table. Seal unused food from dinner preparation in containers or bags and put it away, move the utensil caddy to the center, and set the table. You'll want to locate your lantern before the sun goes down.

Before sitting down to eat, put a pot of water on the stove or over the campfire to heat. It'll be hot when it's time to wash dishes. After dinner, use two plastic washtubs—one for soapy water and one for rinse water—and some elbow grease, and you've got yourself a dishwasher! It's much more fun to wash dishes outdoors while watching chipmunks play than it is at home.

No-Pins Clothesline

To make a No-Pins Clothesline, tie two ropes (or one really long one) around a tree. Twist the length of the ropes together. Tie the new twisted rope around another tree. Stuff the ends of your wet clothes or towels into the loops created by the twisted ropes. You can also air out your sleeping bags on the clothesline when you are sure it isn't going to rain.

🔥 BUILDING A CAMPFIRE

A campfire is one of your best friends when camping. You'll use it to cook food, stay warm, and to sit around at night to tell stories and sing campfire songs. There are several good ways to build a fire.

Even the most experienced mountaineer can't start a fire with just logs. You need to start with smaller fuel. Start with the tinder—that will light the kindling. Then the kindling will light the logs.

Tinder is the first fuel you put in the firebox or fire circle. It should be something small that burns quickly. Twigs, dry grass, pinecones, and even crumpled sheets of newspaper are good tinder.

On top of that put slightly larger pieces of wood that will burn longer. These "kindle" the flame, keeping it going until the large wood catches fire. Bigger twigs and sticks will work.

Next is the wood, usually small logs. Hardwoods such as oak and maple are best for cooking fires. The coals of these woods burn slowly, giving you more cooking time. In many areas, cottonwood and pine are the available wood. Those softwoods burn quickly. If you use them, have all your food ready when you light the fire so you can begin cooking as soon as the coals reach the right stage.

Some places have no wood at all. On the treeless plains, Native Americans and pioneers had to cook over fires made of "buffalo chips" (dry manure). You could use charcoal instead.

Backwoodsmen know how to build different kinds of campfires for different ways of cooking. Here are some you can try.

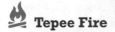 **Tepee Fire**

A tepee fire burns quickly with a lot of heat. It's good for boiling water to cook spaghetti, soup, or vegetables. Put your tinder in the middle and then stand up sticks over it in a tepee shape.

🔥 Log Cabin Fire

A log cabin fire burns down to a thick bed of smoldering coals ideal for cooking feasts on a stick, in aluminum foil, or on a grill. This makes the log cabin fire one of the best fires to cook over. To build a log cabin fire:

1. Make a small pile of tinder, then stack kindling around the outside, leaning the wood toward the center in the shape of a small tepee.

2. Pile logs around the tepee as if you were building a tiny log cabin.

3. As the cabin gets taller, gradually place the logs a little closer to the tepee.

4. Add logs until the cabin is about as tall as your knees.

5. Strike a safety match, which is coated so that it will light only on the striking plate on the matchbox, and carefully light the tinder.

🔥 Pyramid Fire

The Pyramid Fire is similar to the Log Cabin Fire, except the stacks get smaller as it reaches the top.

1. Place two small logs on the ground parallel to each other.

2. Place a layer of small logs or branches on top of them in a row perpendicularly.

3. Add another layer of small branches or logs, in the other direction. Make the layer smaller, so the stack doesn't go all the way out to the edge of the last layer.

4. Do this two or three more times.

5. Light the top of the pyramid on fire, and it will burn downwards onto itself.

🔥 Charcoal Fire

If firewood isn't available, use charcoal piled in a pyramid. Follow the directions on the charcoal bag. Some charcoal requires the use of lighter fluid, while other kinds come ready to light. Ask an adult to apply the lighter fluid. Do not add any fluid after you have struck a match.

Campers have to be patient. It takes a while for the campfire to get to the cooking stage. The time varies with the kind of wood you use, but it is usually 20 to 30 minutes. Even if those you are cooking for are holding their plates, drooling, and asking, "Isn't that fire ready yet?" don't start cooking until the flames die down and just coals are left, or you will burn your food. Set the table and get the ingredients ready while you wait. When the flames die down and the coals glow red with white edges, it's time to cook your grub.

A reflector fire is best for baking. It is
built against the stone or metal wall of
the fire ring. The rocks and metal give
off (reflect) heat long after the fire is out.

FIRE STARTERS

You can use fire starters for your tinder to help get your campfire going.
Try the Newspaper Fire Starter, Pinecone Fire Starter, or Sawdust Fire Starter.

Newspaper Fire Starter

WHAT YOU NEED:

★ Melted wax
★ Newspaper
★ 6 pieces of string, about 2 inches long
   each
★ Scissors
★ Wax paper

1. Melt wax according to directions
   (pages 61–63).

2. Roll up a sheet of newspaper the long way.

3. Every 3 or 4 inches, tie a string around it.

4. Cut the newspaper between the strings, so you have small tied bundles of newspaper.

5. Hold the end of the string and lower the newspaper into the pot of hot wax. When you pull it out of the wax, hold it over the pot for a few seconds until it stops dripping. Then lay it on the wax paper to dry.

6. Trim the string to a few inches.

🔥 Pinecone Fire Starter

WHAT YOU NEED:

- ★ Pinecones
- ★ 1 piece of string, about 10 inches long, for each pinecone
- ★ Newspaper
- ★ Potholder or trivet
- ★ Melted wax

WHAT YOU DO:

1. Tie a piece of string around each pinecone. Leave about a 6-inch tail.

2. Spread some newspaper on a flat surface and place the potholder or trivet on it.

3. Melt wax according to directions (pages 61–63). Using an oven mitt, place the container of melted wax on the potholder.

4. Holding the tail of the string, dip a pinecone into the wax.

5. After the pinecone is coated, place it on the newspaper until it is dry. Repeat for remaining pinecones.

Sawdust Fire Starter

WHAT YOU NEED:

★ Sawdust or newspaper
★ Cardboard egg carton*
★ Melted wax

*Note: Never burn Styrofoam or plastic!

WHAT YOU DO (IF USING NEWSPAPER):

1. Shred the newspaper and fill each egg cup with some of the shredded pieces.

2. Melt wax according to directions (pages 61–63).

3. Carefully pour wax into the newspaper-filled egg carton.

4. Let the fire starter cool and harden.

WHAT YOU DO (IF USING SAWDUST):

1. Melt wax according to directions (pages 61–63).

2. Stir the sawdust into the melted wax.

3. Carefully pour the hot wax-and-sawdust mixture into each cup of the egg carton.

4. Let the fire starter cool and harden.

🔥 MELTING WAX

You can buy wax at a craft store. It comes in blocks. Use ½ pound of wax (also called paraffin) for each set of fire starters. Be careful! Wax catches fire if it gets too hot. Its ability to burn will allow you to start a fire with it later. Have an adult helper with you.

You'll use a double boiler to melt your wax. A double boiler is a special kind of pot. You can buy one at a retail store or at a thrift shop where it will be inexpensive. If you don't have a real double boiler, you can use a saucepan and an empty soup or coffee can that is dry, clean, and free of paper.

WHAT YOU DO:

1. Fill a 2- or 3-quart saucepan about halfway with water.

2. Put it on the stove over high heat until the water comes to a boil. Then turn the heat down to medium-low.

3. Put your solid wax in the top part of the double boiler or in the can. Carefully place this part into the water, making sure water doesn't get in with your wax.

4. Stir the wax gently with a spoon as it melts. When the wax is completely liquid, turn off the stove.

5. Using an oven mitt, remove the can or pot from the water and place it on a potholder. Use the melted wax to make your fire starters.

🔥 COOKING OVER THE FIRE

Many great meals come from cooking over the coals of a fire. After you have burned your fire down, you can place a grill over the coals to cook meat or vegetables. Or you can set a skillet on the grill to cook pancakes or fry bacon. Another option is wrapping your food in tinfoil and placing it directly on the coals. It's a great way to make roasted chicken or baked potatoes. Or you can cook your food on a stick held over the fire, like roasting hotdogs or shish kabobs.

It's fun to cook right over an open fire, but there may be times when you can't have a fire. Maybe there is a forest fire watch prohibiting open campfires or maybe you want to do a cookout in your own backyard or at a nearby park where fires aren't allowed. Gas grills, camp stoves, and charcoal grills are other great options for outdoor cooking.

🔥 PUTTING OUT THE FIRE

After your meal and before you leave your cooking site, you must put out the campfire. Follow these simple steps.

1. Use a stick to spread the coals into a thin layer.

NIGHTLIGHTS

You'll enjoy a battery-operated lantern to shed light on bedtime reading or game playing. Headlamps—which are flashlights you strap to your head—are great for reading. You can use a headlamp or a flashlight placed near the door to help guide you on those middle-of-the-night trips to the outhouse.

2. Sprinkle water or dirt over all of the coals. Warning: Don't pour a large amount of water on the coals all at once! It makes steam that could burn you or others standing nearby.

3. Stir the coals and add more water or dirt until the coals are cool enough to touch. An adult can help you with this.

SETTING UP YOUR TENT

One of the first things you do after you pick a campsite is pitch your tent. Here are some rules to follow to help you.

The tent should be on a level spot. Just a slight incline will make you feel like you're going to slide into a heap at the bottom of the tent. Many campgrounds have a level place outlined with logs and filled with smooth dirt. If yours doesn't, get on your hands and knees and clear the area of rocks and sticks. Remember the story of *The Princess and the Pea*?

Even little lumps under your bed will keep you tossing and turning all night!

Once you've picked a level spot and cleared the area, put down your ground cloth and set up your tent. Blow up air mattresses and arrange them, or foam pads, to suit your group. Put sleeping bags on top of the mattresses or pads, and clothes where you can reach them, but not against the walls of the tent. If there is rain, it will seep through the tent walls wherever anything is touching.

Choosing Your Tent

Whatever size and style you choose, the most important function of the tent is to keep you dry. A rain fly will direct moisture away from the tent. A sheet of heavyweight plastic spread under the tent, called a ground cloth, will keep the floor dry and clean. Buy it by the yard at hardware, home, and garden stores.

When choosing a tent, look for:

- [ ] A rain fly
- [ ] Two layers of fabric in places where poles or ropes will attach
- [ ] Heavy-duty, double-stitched seams
- [ ] Screens to keep out crawling, flying, and buzzing critters
- [ ] A small porch for storage or sitting
- [ ] Room for relaxing, playing games, or reading on rainy days

Make Your Own Tent

Eventually you'll want a manufactured tent because of its useful features, but you can make your own tent for clear, warm nights.

1. Find two trees about ten feet apart.

2. Tie each end of a rope to the trees, about four feet from the ground. The rope should be tight so it doesn't sag.

3. Throw a tarp or old blanket over the rope so that half of the material hangs down on either side.

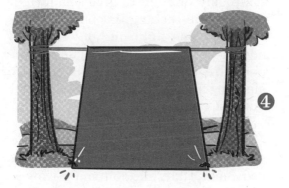

4. Using tent stakes (available at outdoor shops) or pegs made from branches, stake the four corners to the ground. Add another stake between the corners on each side.

SLEEPING BAGS

A tent will keep you dry but it won't keep you warm. That's the job of your camp bed—the sleeping bag. Sleep sacks come in two basic styles: rectangular and mummy. Many campers consider the rectangular bag more comfortable. It's roomy enough to give some wiggle room. Some rectangular bags have two top flaps, one light and one heavy. By adding or tossing them off as the temperature changes, you will find your sleeping bag not too hot, not too cold, but just right.

Mummy bags are fitted to the human shape. They hold the camper, and her body heat, tight like a mummy. They are usually the choice of backpack campers because they tend to be lighter weight than rectangular ones. Both rectangular and mummy bags can be found in youth, adult, and tall-adult sizes.

Check the tag on your sleeping bag for its temperature rating. It will be a number with a degree symbol. If the number is 0 degrees, the bag will keep you warm as long as the temperature doesn't dip below 0. If most of your camping will be done during the summer or on a tropical beach, that bag may be too warm. One with a temperature rating of 35 degrees may be a better choice. Mountain campers need warmer bags (with lower temperature ratings) for cold, high-altitude nights.

Also look at what material fills your bag. Those filled with goose down are toasty warm, lightweight, and more expensive than others. Some synthetic fillings such as polyester, Polarguard, and Thinsulate are also warm but cost less and are easier to wash.

Keep these things in mind when selecting a sleeping bag:

★ Washability
★ Durable shell
★ Drawstring around the top to help keep in your body heat
★ Fabric layer inside the zipper
★ Temperature rating that suits the type of camping you plan to do

★   Filling that keeps you warm and fits
     your budget

Make Your Own Sleeping Bag

Until you purchase a sleeping bag, make
one.

1. Start with two blankets.

2. Place the left half of one blanket over
    the right half of the other.

3. Fold the left half of the bottom blan-
    ket over the two blanket layers you
    already have and then the right half
    of the last blanket over the stack.

4. Carefully pin together with large
    safety or blanket pins.

5. Now fold up one end and pin it.

6. Crawl in and sleep snug as a skunk in
    a woodpile!

Sleeping Pads

Sleeping pads go under your sleeping bag, providing a layer between you and the cold, hard, sometimes rocky ground. They keep you warmer, drier, and more comfortable. Your sleeping pad might be an inflatable air mattress or a foam pad. Some versatile pads can be folded and slipped into a fabric frame, forming a camp chair for daytime use.

KEEPING CLEAN

When you're out in the woods you can get dusty, dirty, and sweaty. If your campsite doesn't have a shower facility, you have to figure out a way to keep clean.

Camp stores sell five-gallon collapsible plastic water jugs. Fill one with water before you leave home or with treated water in camp. Tie a rope on the handle and hang the jug from a tree branch near the edge of your campsite. If you dangle it over a vegetated area (one covered with plant growth), you won't make mud when you use it.

Put a bar of soap in a mesh vegetable bag or an old nylon stocking and tie it onto the jug handle so it hangs down near the spout. Now everything you need to wash your face and hands is right where you need it. Take a cup and your camper cleanup kit to the area and you can brush your teeth while you're there.

CLEAN WATER

The main ingredient to any cleanup is water. The water in most campgrounds is treated and safe to use and to drink. However, if there is no piped-in water, you may have to get it from a creek or lake. You can't tell by looking whether or not the water has harmful bacteria or teeny "bugs" in it. To make water safe, boil it for ten minutes. That will kill anything that could make you sick. You can also use water filters and treatment tablets that can be found in camping stores.

Camp stores sell solar showers, but you can also make your own. Practiced campers can shower and wash their hair with less than two gallons of water. You may not be that fast, but you can at least rinse off the dust. One trick is to wet your hair down and apply shampoo before you start.

Hang a dark, heavy-duty trash bag on a sturdy branch. Make sure it is in a place that gets lots of sun. Pour two gallons of water into the bag. Let the sun heat it for several hours. When you are ready to shower, wet your hair and lather it with soap. Then poke a fork into the bottom of the bag and wash and rinse fast under the water that drains out. Experiment with stopping the water flow momentarily by pinching the open area with your fingers or a clothespin. Warning: sometimes you have to rinse with cold water.

POOPING IN THE WOODS

If there are bathroom facilities where you are camping, use those. If not, you can pee behind any tree or rock big enough to give you privacy. Pooping is a different story. You'll need to dig a pit toilet. Why? Poop pollutes water with germs that are harmful to everyone downstream. And it isn't pleasant to stumble onto someone else's mess in the backcountry! Properly disposing of your own body waste is just plain good "forest keeping."

You may not feel comfortable asking a forest ranger the right way to poop in the woods, so read on:

1. Using your trowel, dig a hole 6 to 8 inches deep and a little wider. Pile the loose dirt to one side. The hole should be at least 100 feet from any water or any place where rain might run off into a lake or stream below.

2. Squat over the hole and do your business.

3. Use toilet paper if you have it, leaves if you don't. Put paper in the hole unless the rules at your campsite say used toilet paper must be carried out. If so, put it in a plastic bag and seal it tight.

4. Using the trowel, cover everything with the dirt that you dug from the hole.

KEEP IT GREEN

Green camping is earth-friendly camping. It means you leave little or no trace that you have camped in a place. Old camp manuals taught campers how to haul rocks to make a fire ring and cut trees to make comfy furniture. There are too many campers today to continue camping that way. Resources would soon be depleted if we all used whatever we pleased.

Here are some earth-friendly ways you can camp:

1. Keep a clean camp. Dispose of all waste in the campground's trash and recycle containers or pack it out.

2. Clean up any trash left by others. You shouldn't have to, but you'll be glad you did. The general rule is: "Leave it better than you found it."

3. Leave rocks, logs, dirt, or plants where they are. You came to visit nature—leave it natural.

4. Use soap and "the bathroom" far away from bodies of water. If you don't, the soap and human waste will be washed into the water with the next rain. Both are harmful to the fish who live there and the animals and people who live downstream.

5. Don't have a campfire every night. The wood you use for a campfire could make a home for insects and small animals. When left to decay on the forest floor, it feeds the earth.

Enjoy a campfire occasionally, but make it a special event.

When you put together all the living things that are together in one place, you have what is called an ecosystem. Different plants and animals grow in different ecosystems. Cactus and lizards are at home in the dry heat of the desert, but polar bears and low-growing alpine plants prefer the cold, windswept tundra.

Whatever ecosystem you get to camp in, remember, it's somebody's home. Treat it better than you would your own, and help keep the wilderness wild.

DRAW A PICTURE OF YOUR CAMPSITE HERE

IDEAS FOR KEEPING CAMP CLEAN

THINGS TO REMEMBER NEXT TIME YOU PITCH CAMP

CHAPTER THREE

AND

FIRST AID

C amping and hiking outdoors can be a lot of fun. It can also be dangerous. You have to be careful when you are exposed to the elements, insects, campfires, hiking trails, and other things where you could get hurt. Use caution in your activities and always keep a first aid kit handy.

FIRST AID KIT

Your first aid kit contains everything you need to doctor the little cuts, bumps, and bruises that happen on almost every camping trip. When someone's ear is scratched by a fishhook, a knee is scraped by a rock, or a foot gets a blister from hiking all the way to a cave and back, you'll be able to clean up the injury and ease the pain if you have the following things packed and available:

☐ Moist towelettes to clean wounds
☐ Bandages to keep small cuts clean and dry

☐ Gauze and adhesive tape to keep larger wounds clean and dry

☐ Moleskin to keep shoes from rubbing on blisters

☐ Small scissors to cut gauze, tape, and moleskin

☐ Aspirin or other fever and pain reducers to ease pain

☐ Antibiotic cream to disinfect wounds

Your adult helper should have a first aid kit, too, to doctor bigger hurts. And don't forget to take and use sunscreen and insect repellent. They might keep you from having to use the first aid kit at all.

STAYING FOUND

Being lost in the forest can be scary. There are no street signs and no familiar buildings to help you get back to camp. Not only that, but one tree can look pretty much like another when you are out and about. Here are some simple things to do that will help you stay found when hiking:

★ Always let someone know where you
   are going.
★ Never hike alone.
★ Stay on trails.
★ Pay attention to the land you are
   walking through. Occasionally turn
   around and look behind you so you'll
   know what to look for on the way back.
★ Watch for landmarks: bent trees, oddly
   shaped rocks, bear caves, trees that
   have fallen across the stream.

★ Carry a whistle and a mirror. The whistle can be heard much farther than your voice can. If you flash the mirror in the sunlight, especially if you are high on a hill, it can be seen for miles and miles.

★ Carry an area map with you. Before setting out, sit down with an adult and look at the map. Locate roads, rivers, forests, and any landmarks you can see. Turn the map so that the markers on your map line up with what you see. Mark your campsite and the trail you are going to follow.

★ Always carry water and a little snack with you. You'll enjoy taking a snack break, and, if you get lost, it could make you a lot more comfortable while you wait to be found.

If you think you are lost, it is important to stay calm and stay where you are. You will be tempted to try to find your own way out, but if you are scared, you may run miles off the course or trek out even farther in the wrong direction. Your fellow campers will look for you in the area they think you went, so hug a tree and stay put.

Blow your whistle in a series of three blows every few minutes until you are found. If you must leave the area—for instance, in order to climb a tree or nearby hill to signal with your mirror—mark your trail so you can get back and others will know how to find you.

Trail Marking

What you use to mark your trail depends on what's available; it may be grass tips tied together, stacked stones, or arranged twigs.

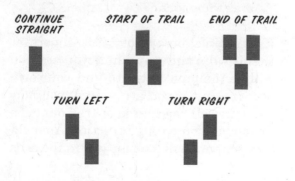

CONTINUE STRAIGHT   START OF TRAIL   END OF TRAIL

TURN LEFT   TURN RIGHT

Make sure the trail markings you make are noticeable and distinguishable from the natural surroundings.

You can make up other markings, such as a number of rocks to show how many steps to go in the direction of the marker, or one that indicates that the hiker turned

HOW LONG TILL SUNDOWN?

Here is a little trick to help you determine how long it is until sunset:

1. Hold your arm straight out in front of you.

2. Put your hand out, as if you are shaking hands (thumb on top), so you can count how many fingers of sky there are between land and the sun. Remember, never look directly at the sun.

3. One finger width measures about 15 minutes, so 4 fingers mean it's about an hour until the sun goes down.

around. But make sure most people can figure them out if you are really lost.

MAPS

How far is it from the trailhead to Twin Owls Rock?

Do you cross a stream, a marsh, or a rock-slide when walking from Mount Casper to Gold Rush Gulch?

Is Sunrise Campground closer to Rainbow Pond or Twin Owls Rock?

If you are at Big Bear Cave, how far is it to the nearest restroom?

If you are at Gold Rush Gulch and your car is parked at the Shaggy Moose parking lot, what direction do you walk in to get there?

Maps are a great resource to keep you safe and aware of your surroundings while camping. A favorite thing to do while camping is to explore the surrounding area and go on hikes. The more you know about hiking, the more you'll enjoy it. You should know how to read a map and take one with you before heading for the trailhead. This will help keep you safe.

You'll find there are many kinds of maps, but you'll want to locate a trail map at a bookstore, recreation center, outdoor shop, or park-service information station. Once you have a trail map, review it. Is there a creek along your path? How far is it to the cave you've heard about? How long would it take you to get there?

Answers to these questions can be found on the legend.

The legend contains the map's scale, the directional compass, and the symbol library.

What's the scale? The scale is how much real space is represented on the map. If one mile of real distance is represented by three inches on the map, you can measure the trail you want to take. If, on the map, the trail is six inches long, and three inches represents one mile, then how long is the trail? (Answer: two miles)

The directional compass shows you which way north, south, east, and west are on the map. North is usually at the top of the map.

The symbol library explains what each symbol on the map means. From it, you can figure out which line is a road, a trail, or a stream, where the campgrounds are, and, just in case you need one, the

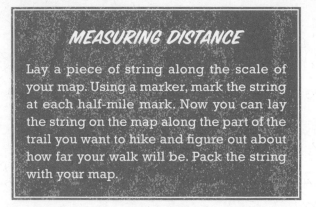

MEASURING DISTANCE

Lay a piece of string along the scale of your map. Using a marker, mark the string at each half-mile mark. Now you can lay the string on the map along the part of the trail you want to hike and figure out about how far your walk will be. Pack the string with your map.

location of the nearest restroom. It will also indicate the trailhead, which is where the trail begins.

WATER, WATER, WATER

Human beings cannot live without water. Being sure you have safe water when camping is essential to your survival. Here are some questions and answers about water:

Can I drink from the stream?
No. Water is often polluted by users

upstream. Besides, it's home (and bathroom) to fish, beaver, and other critters.

How much water do I need?
In hot weather, half a quart for each mile you hike. In cold weather, half a pint for each mile you hike.

Why the difference?
You lose more water through perspiration in hot weather than you do in cold weather. What you lost must be replaced.

How should I carry my water?
Carry it in a plastic container with a top that closes tightly. You may want one large bottle or two smaller ones. Some like containers that hook onto a belt while others prefer one on a strap to loop across their body. Some water bottle models have hooks and straps and can be carried either way. There are even soft water carriers you wear on your back— they come with a long straw you can use to slurp cold water as you tramp along the trail!

I'm going on a long hike and can't carry that much water. If I shouldn't drink the river water, what do I do?

Water tablets and portable water filters are available at outdoor and sports shops. Use them to treat river or stream water. They clean the bad stuff out, making the water safe to drink. Ask the salesclerk to show you how they work.

EMERGENCY

If you are lost in the woods or a rainstorm and need shelter for the night, first look for a natural shelter. It might be an overhanging rock or bushes that form a curve. Or you can make a simple lean-to shelter using dental floss and a solar blanket. Put the back of the lean-to into the wind.

Here is a list of other things to take with you when camping. These will serve you well in case of an emergency. Assemble these items in a sealable plastic bag:

- ☐ whistle
- ☐ map
- ☐ shatterproof metal mirror
- ☐ solar blanket
- ☐ 10 feet of bright-colored plastic tape
- ☐ matches/strike strip in a waterproof container
- ☐ fire starters
- ☐ dental floss
- ☐ candy bar

READING THE WEATHER

Bad weather can change you from a happy camper into a damp duck in just a few minutes. Experienced campers and hikers keep an eye on the weather. They start watching the forecast days before their trip and keep watching the sky for clues to possible weather changes while they are walking. Moody weather doesn't necessarily mean you must cancel your trip. Many people prefer hiking in a drizzle to hiking in the hot sun. It just means you must be prepared and take enough gear to protect yourself.

If you notice these things, put on your hiking boots. The weather should be good for being outdoors.

1. A mellow, yellow sunset or sunrise.
2. A gentle wind.
3. No clouds, high clouds, thin clouds, or few clouds.
4. A clear blue sky.

But, if you see these things, consider staying home with a good book.

1. A red sunrise.
2. A sudden drop in temperature.
3. Increasing winds.
4. Low clouds, dark clouds, or fast-moving clouds.
5. A ring around the sun or moon.

PREVENTING HEAT EXHAUSTION

L et's face it. When any person—young or old, male or female—gets too hot, they sweat. Sweat evaporates and cools the skin. Sweat is a loss of fluid. If fluids aren't replaced, sweating decreases and the body gets hotter.

Heat exhaustion has the following symptoms: you feel faint and sick to your stomach, your skin is pale and clammy, and you have a headache or feel weak. What should you do? Stop walking, lie down in the shade, put your feet up, rest, and drink water. If you have salt with you, put a little in your water. The salt will allow your body to retain fluid better. The water will lower your internal temperature. When you feel better, start back. Keep replenishing your body fluids by drinking water. If you become very dehydrated, it would be a good idea to see a doctor when you get back to civilization.

PREVENTING BLISTERS

I t pays to be aware of your "doggies" (feet). You can learn to prevent most blisters. While hiking, if you feel a spot on your foot getting hot, stop. Your foot is being rubbed raw. If it continues, a blister could form. Just cut a piece of moleskin a little bigger than the sore spot and stick it over the area. The soft moleskin will probably prevent a blister, and you'll walk a lot more comfortably.

If you find you already have a blister, don't pop it. Cover it with moleskin that has a small hole cut to fit over the blister, or cover it with a bandage; leave it until the body reabsorbs the fluid. If the blister does rupture, keep it clean so it won't become infected. Wash it with mild soap and water, then bandage it. If a blister becomes red, a doctor should look at it.

After hiking all day, coddle your feet with a warm-water bath. Then dry them well, especially between those tootsies! Put fresh moleskin or bandages on any sore places. Cover with clean cotton socks.

AVOIDING BUGS

The best thing to do about bugs is to avoid them. That's not so easy when you

YELLOW JACKET

MOSQUITO

TICK

WASP

BUMBLEBEE

are camping and hiking around in their living room. Bees, yellow jackets, and wasps usually bug you just when you annoy them, but ticks and mosquitoes think you are dinner delivered on a hiking boot! No time outdoors will be free of bugs unless you are hiking in the snow. So, what should you do?

1. Dress for bug defense. Wear long pants and tuck them into heavy socks. Fashion goes out the window when it competes with pesky bugs. You can also wear a lightweight shirt with long sleeves to protect your arms. Dark clothes attract insects so wear light colors.

2. Wear insect repellent. The most effective insect repellents contain a chemical known as DEET. If you use these, follow the directions on the container. Keep DEET-containing solutions tightly closed, sealed in a sealable plastic bag, and carried in a separate pocket of your pack. They can melt down some plastics and will ruin your camera. Many people are allergic to DEET or don't want to use chemicals. There are natural bug repellents like citronella oil that can be used instead. They are not usually as effective as DEET but still offer some protection.

3. Treat bug bites. Baking soda mixed with a little water is a simple itch stop for mosquito bites, and you can use it for toothpaste, too. But don't use it on bee or wasp stings. They need something acidic, like lemon juice. There are also some easy-traveling sticks of stop-itch available, as well as the traditional calamine lotion.

Enjoy the insects you see from afar.

DRAGONFLY

FIREFLY

LADYBUG

TICK, TICK, TICK

Ticks are plentiful in many areas. They are small eight-legged bugs with hard flat bodies. They bite and suck blood and can also transmit such diseases as Rocky Mountain Spotted Fever and Lyme Disease. Both of these can be treated, but they can turn serious and you are better off to avoid them. Wear insect repellent and dress for bug defense. Occasionally, check your clothing and flick off any ticks you find.

When you get home after hiking in tick country, have someone check through your hair and on your scalp for ticks. You can check your body. Check especially in tight dark places like armpits and groin. If rashes, headaches, fever, or severe muscle aches develop a few days after hiking, head for the doctor for some tick treatment. Be sure to tell her you were in a "ticky" area.

AVOIDING POISONOUS PLANTS

One of the main reasons people camp is to enjoy nature. But not all of nature is so enjoyable—there are poisonous plants that can drive a camper crazy. A camper who brushes past poison ivy, poison oak, or poison sumac may not even notice . . . until twenty-four to forty-eight hours later. That's when the itchy, blistery, red rash shows up. Avoiding these villainous bushes is the best defense. Watch out for these and step around them.

If you do come in contact with the bad guys, follow these steps:

1. Wash the plant's oils off of you as soon as possible. Remove and wash clothing that may have come in contact with the plant, handling it as little as possible.

2. Clean the contaminated skin area with alcohol. There are individually packaged alcohol-soaked towelettes available.

3. When a rash develops, dab with calamine lotion.

WRITE ABOUT THE WEATHER ON YOUR CAMPING TRIP HERE

DRAW ANY BUGS YOU SAW WHILE CAMPING

DRAW A MAP OF YOUR CAMPSITE AND SURROUNDING AREA

CHAPTER FOUR

CAMPFIRE

Whether you're cooking in aluminum foil, a paper bag, or a pot, the one thing you absolutely need is heat. Your kitchen at home probably has a few different ways of heating things—the stovetop, oven, microwave, toaster, and so on. You can use a variety of heating methods at camp, too. Most camp cooks, in both the backyard and backwoods, like to cook over an old-fashioned campfire, but they also enjoy the convenience of a charcoal fire, gas-powered camp stove, or backyard grill.

SHOPPING

Even when you plan and pack carefully, every once in a while you will probably forget something. If you're left without some supplies, improvise! A few layers of tin foil can be folded into a bowl, plastic bags can make plates, and clean hands can do a lot of things silverware can.

Many campsites and parks have general stores with the bare essentials. Pay a visit to replace things that simply have no substitute like marshmallows and chocolate bars.

Once you've chosen recipes for your camping trip, make a shopping list from the list of ingredients. Before you shop, consider how you will store your food.

PACKING FOOD

Fresh meats and fish should be bought the day of the trip, kept really cold, and eaten that day or the next. Refrigerated food should be packed in a camp ice chest with ice or several large ice packs. Not all camp ice chests come with a drain, but try to get one that does. Otherwise, you'll have to take everything out of the chest each day when it's time to drain the water and add more ice.

Bacon, lunchmeats, and other meats containing preservatives can be kept for a few days if ice is replenished daily. They should be stored in sealable plastic bags. Cheese, eggs, and fresh veggies can also be kept for several days.

If your trip is for more than a day or two, most of the food you pack should be the kind that can keep on a shelf for a long time. After the ice in your ice chest has melted away you can eat well for weeks with some flour, sugar, grains (such as rice), pasta, nuts, bread, dry breakfast cereals, canned meats and fish, fruits and vegetables, instant milk, soups, sauces, and freeze-dried camp meals.

KEEPING FOOD COLD

Milk, cheese, meat, and some other foods must stay cold until you cook or eat them, or else they can make you sick. Other things, like fruit and drinks, just taste better cold. Chocolate bars may not normally need to be refrigerated, but they'll be chocolate soup if packed in a hot car and not kept cool!

You can carry food that needs to be kept cool to your cook site in a plastic ice chest or insulated container with some ice packs or resealable plastic bags filled with ice. If you plan on having leftovers, bring enough ice to keep extra food cold until it's eaten.

Natural Refrigeration

Once you get to your campsite, you may
be able to use natural refrigeration to
keep some foods cool. If there is a lake
or stream nearby (that's not too deep or
too swift), bundle up your fruit in a plastic sack, bucket, or crate and set it into
a slow, shallow spot in the water. Anchor
your container with rocks or lash it to
a tree so it doesn't wash away. Use this
method for foods that can be peeled and
the peel thrown away—never eat the part
that touches the water. So, for example,
bananas or string cheese sealed in plastic
are okay, but apples or lunchmeat aren't,
unless they're tightly sealed in plastic
bags or containers.

SAFE WATER

Rivers, lakes, and oceans are wonderful places to dip your feet, cool
a watermelon, or sit by. But no matter
how refreshing the water looks, never
drink it! Ocean water is too salty to drink,

and most lakes and rivers carry bacteria called giardia (gee-ARE-dee-a) which can make you very sick.

Many parks have pumps or spigots with drinkable water, but unless you know this ahead of time, it's best to bring your own water or a way to treat unsafe water.

Bottled water is widely available. But with all the cooking, washing, and drinking you'll be doing, it can get expensive. Most grocery, retail, or outdoor stores sell reusable water bottles or canteens to fill at home and take with you.

There are many options for water treatment, including chemicals and filters. The cheapest way to purify water is to boil it for ten minutes.

CAMPFIRES

Campers do it. Cowpokes do it. City people sometimes travel miles to do it. They all cook over a campfire.

Sometimes they roast marshmallows in the middle of a forest. Other times they grill salmon in a city park. Whatever they are preparing, it always tastes better cooked out-of-doors. Fresh air and the smell of wood smoke stir the appetite. Without refrigerators, stoves, or microwaves, outdoor cooks can create great meals—sometimes even better than the ones at home.

♨ Rules of Campfire Cooking

Being smart about fire safety helps keep everyone safe.

★ Always have an adult helper with you when you're using fire.

★ Never leave a fire unattended.

★ Build fires in a pit, an existing fire ring, or a fire ring you make with larger rocks, cinder blocks, or bricks placed in a circle on flat ground. Put stoves, grills, and other heat sources on flat, heat-resistant surfaces that are clear of grass, pinecones, paper, or anything else that could catch fire.

★ A smaller fire is easier to control and is better for cooking.

PUTTING OUT THE FIRE

When you're ready to leave your campsite or turn in for the night, use your shovel and bucket and put out the fire. With the shovel or a stick, spread the coals into a thin, even layer. Dribble water, dirt, or sand onto the coals. Pour slowly! Dumping water on all at once will fling sparks into the air and out of the fire ring. It could even burn you with steam. Besides, a slow dribble on the fire makes a cool sizzle. When the coals appear to be out, carefully stir them, and then repeat the process.

★ Never use outside equipment inside. Camp stoves and the stoves used in this book are all meant to be used outdoors.

★ Always keep a shovel and a bucket of water or sand nearby. You'll need these to put out the fire when you're finished cooking or in case of an emergency.

★ Make sure the fire is completely out when you're finished. Ask an adult to check.

Notes on Campfire Cooking

Pitching Camp (page 50), has directions for building different types of campfires. Remember, altitude (how high up you are from sea level) affects cooking time. If two people cook the same food over identical fires—one on an ocean beach and the other high in the mountains—the chef on the beach will finish cooking first. Also, fires made of different woods burn differently. Some burn hotter or faster than others. The cooking times given in this book are averages. Your food may cook a little faster or a little slower than the time listed. Pay attention while you're cooking so things don't burn.

There are a lot of ways to do your camp cooking. In this chapter you will learn

COOKING WITH CHARCOAL

Charcoal is another kind of fuel. You can make a charcoal fire in your backyard or at a campsite and cook your food over it on an existing grill or one you make yourself. Charcoal lights faster than wood, so you only need tinder (usually lighter fluid or paper) and the main fuel (charcoal briquettes). Remember to build the fire in the body of the grill and don't forget your fire safety rules! A charcoal fire usually starts out with smoke, then flames. When the flames die down, the coals glow red. Then they turn white on the edges. When the edges of about three-quarters of the coals are white, you're ready to cook.

how to cook on grills and camp stoves, over the fire on a stick, directly on the coals, in a pit, and in a solar oven.

GRILLS AND CAMP STOVES

Gas-powered stoves and grills adjust easily for cooking from low (for keeping soup warm) to high (for boiling water), and anything in between. Grills come in many different shapes and sizes, and use different fuel types like propane or kerosene. All have wire racks for cooking meat, vegetables, or a dessert.

Camp stoves are portable, gas-powered stoves that have one to three burners. They work best when you are cooking something in a pot or pan like on your stovetop at home.

When using your camp grill, remove the wire rack and build the fire inside the grill body. On the underside of many grills, there is a vent that opens and closes with a handle—open this vent before starting the fire. When you're finished with the fire, close the vent to cut off the supply of oxygen.

Using a stick or shovel, spread the coals across the bottom of the grill and carefully set the grate on top. Placing a lid over the grill will speed up the cooking time. If the lid has a vent, use it to adjust your fire: The wider open it is, the faster and hotter the fire burns. Less open allows a slower burning, cooler fire. Close it and your fire goes out.

🔥 Make a Tin-Can Grill

A tin-can grill is easy and inexpensive to make and can be recycled, thrown away, or reused. Be careful with the can, as the edges are sharp and the metal gets hot. You'll need an adult helper.

WHAT YOU NEED:

☐   a large, clean, empty 2-pound coffee can

☐   heavy work gloves
☐   tin snips
☐   dirt or sand
☐   aluminum foil
☐   metal grate (racks used for cooling
      cookies work well)

WHAT YOU DO:

1. Put on gloves!

2. Using the tin snips, cut
   a line from the open
   end of the can towards the bottom,
   stopping 3 inches from the end.

3. Make another cut just like this,
   2 inches away from the first cut.
   Repeat until you get back to the first
   cut and the circle is completed. Pull
   the 2-inch strips away from the center.
   You should have a basket-like holder
   and access to the center of the can.

4. Pour dirt or sand into the center of the
   can, about 2 inches deep.

5. Line the center and strips with heavy aluminum foil, creating a big silver bowl. Be careful! The strips are sharp.

6. Place the grate on the strips and carefully push it down so it is level.

7. Remove the grate and place the grill on the ground in a space free of twigs, leaves, or anything else that could burn.

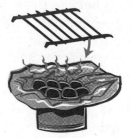 

8. Build a charcoal fire right in the grill or use a shovel to carefully transfer hot coals from an existing fire.

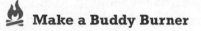

Make a Buddy Burner

A buddy burner is a small, easy-to-make stove perfect for cooking small amounts of food for one or two hungry campers. You make a buddy burner in a can. You'll want to make yours at least a day in advance.

WHAT YOU NEED:

- ☐ short, squat cans (like tuna or pineapple cans)
- ☐ corrugated cardboard, free from bright inks, wax, or tape
- ☐ scissors
- ☐ melted wax (pages 61–63)

WHAT YOU DO:

1. Cut strips of cardboard that are as tall as your can is high. Cut across the

corrugation, so you can see the holes in the edge of the cardboard.

2. Roll up the cardboard and fit it snugly into the can. Cut a thin strip of cardboard ½ inch longer than the can is tall. Put this strip in the spiral so it sticks out of the can. This is your wick.

3. Pour melted wax into the can, almost covering the cardboard. Ta-da! You've made a buddy burner. When you're ready to cook simply light the wick!

A buddy burner should last for about an hour. When finished, cover your buddy burner with a piece of foil larger than the mouth of the burner to put the fire out. Don't move the burner until the wax is hard and cool.

A simple recipe you can make using a buddy burner is toast. Using tongs, just hold a piece of bread above your buddy burner until it's done.

 COOKING ON A STICK

Roasting a hot dog on a stick over the fire is about as "camp cooking" as it gets! Just remember once you build your fire to let it burn down so you are cooking over coals, not over open flames. Otherwise your food will burn, or be burned on the outside and raw on the inside. Use sticks that are long enough to keep your food close to the fire but your hands and face at a safe distance. Consider wearing oven mitts to protect your hands. Hold the food low enough over the coals to cook, but not so low that it burns. Turn it often.

Chapter 6, **Camp Crafts,** has instructions on making the perfect cooking stick from wood (page 208) or making a cooking stick from a coat hanger (page 209). You can also buy cooking sticks at outdoor and sporting goods stores.

♨ COOKING ON THE COALS

Some food works well cooked directly on the coals. This book has recipes for old-fashioned tin foil dinners and barbecued chicken breasts that are wrapped in foil pouches and nestled into the coals to cook. Use oven mitts and tongs to place your food in and out of the coals and be careful not to get burned.

🔥 COOKING IN A CAN

You can use a can as a pot to cook in over the fire or on a stove or grill. Use a clean, paper-free can of any size. If cooking over a fire, set the can into the coals. For best results, balance it on three rocks. If the food needs to be covered as it cooks, cover the can with aluminum foil or turn a larger can upside down over it. After dinner toss the can in the trash or recycle it.

🔥 COOKING IN A PIT

Hot coals buried under dirt create a toasty pit that you can cook food in. When you want to cook in a pit, check the campground rules—some places don't allow you to dig a hole or make a fire ring. To use this method of cooking you have to plan ahead. Some pit cooking recipes take half a day.

1. Dig a hole 2 to 3 times the size of your cooking containers. Keep the dirt. Build a fire in the pit. Use medium-width logs as your main fuel. Keep adding logs as your fire burns. This takes about an hour. By then your pit should be almost filled with coals.

2. While the fire is burning, get your food prepared. Food should be placed in a Dutch oven or foil packets. When you are ready to transfer the food to the cooking pit, ask an adult helper to carefully push the coals to the side of the pit using a shovel.

3. Put your dinner in the pit (don't let foil packets touch each other) and cover them with about 2 to 3 inches of hot coals. Lay foil across the top and cover it with a 3-inch layer of dirt.

4. When your food is cooked, have an adult helper uncover the pit with the shovel. To get out the packets, scoop well under them with a shovel, being

careful not to break the foil. Using tongs or gloves, shake off packets and open up the foil. Be careful: your food will be very hot!

🔥 COOKING IN A SOLAR OVEN

There's another source of heat you might not have thought of for cooking. What is it? The sun! You can harness the energy of the sun through a solar oven.

WHAT YOU NEED:

- ☐ 2 cardboard boxes (1 should be small enough to fit inside the other with about 2 to 3 inches of space on each side)
- ☐ piece of cardboard larger than the top of the larger box
- ☐ white Elmer's glue (non-toxic)
- ☐ aluminum foil
- ☐ black construction paper
- ☐ newspaper
- ☐ stapler
- ☐ clear plastic wrap

WHAT YOU DO:

1. Place the large box over the piece of cardboard and trace the size. Then draw a line 2 inches larger in each direction. Cut out the larger shape.

2. Using the glue, cover one side of your cardboard rectangle with aluminum foil. Rub out the wrinkles, making it as smooth as possible. This will be your reflector. Set it aside for now.

3. Place black construction paper in the bottom of the small box.

4. Line all sides of the inside of the small box with foil. Fold the foil over the top edges to keep it in place.

5. Crumple newspaper into a 2- to 3-inch layer in the bottom of the larger box.

6. Set the small box into the larger one. Stuff the spaces in between the two boxes with crumpled newspaper.

7. Staple one side of the reflector to the back of the large box. Your reflector should be able to stand up on its own. If it won't stay up at about a 45-degree angle, try using a pencil, ruler, or dowel to prop it up.

8. Let the oven sit with the reflector facing the sun for about 30 minutes before putting the food inside. When the food is inside, cover the oven opening with plastic wrap to keep the heat in.

The best time to cook with your solar oven is between 10:00 a.m. and 3:00 p.m. Solar ovens are great for fixing lunch.

BEWARE OF BEARS!

Take extra care if you are in country where bears live. Follow these rules to stay safe.

1. NEVER feed bears. When a bear thinks of people as a food source, she will keep coming back and become a problem bear.

2. Don't keep food inside your tent. If a bear smells your candy bar, the tent walls won't keep him out!

3. If your campground provides lockers, store your food there, or in the trunk of your car. Or, tie it in a bear bag—a

bundle that you raise high into the trees on a rope.

4. Clean up after you cook. Don't leave a mess around after a meal. Store garbage in sealed garbage cans or containers.

5. Don't sleep in clothes you cooked in. They retain the smell of the meal you made and that scent could tickle the taste buds of a hungry bear.

CAMP CLEANUP

After devouring your meal, it's time to clean up—wash dishes, throw away garbage, store food, and set aside recycling. Any time you leave your campsite or go to bed, your space should be spotless. Litter ruins nature for others and invites unwanted visitors like insects and bears. The good news is that cleanup is much more fun in the wilderness than at home!

RECIPES

Rise 'n' Shine Breakfast

Good Morning Sunshine
French Toast

Creamy Dip in a Bread Bowl

Old-Fashioned Tinfoil Dinners

Hawaiian Dinners

Barbecue Chicken

Hearty Chili

Veggie Pie

Moose Kabobs

Grilled Asparagus

Stuffed Mushrooms

Apple Stampede

Wild Chocolate Cake

Orange Cakes

Oatmeal Snacks

S'mores

🔥 Rise 'n' Shine Breakfast

Cook in a paper bag on the coals or on the grill

WHAT YOU NEED:

A DRY, SMALL LUNCH-SIZED BROWN PAPER BAG
2 TO 3 STRIPS BACON
1 TO 2 EGGS
SALT AND PEPPER TO TASTE

WHAT YOU DO:

1. Line the bottom of your bag with the bacon.

2. Crack the eggs on top of the bacon. If you prefer your eggs scrambled, break them into a resealable plastic bag, add some salt and pepper, and squish them around before pouring them on top of the bacon.

3. Fold the top of the bag down three or four turns, stopping before you reach

the food. Spear through the folded part of the bag with a stick and dangle the bag over hot coals. Or you can put the closed bag bacon-side-down on the grill.

Why it works: Grease from the bacon coats the bag and keeps it from catching fire!

Good Morning Sunshine French Toast

Cook on the grill

WHAT YOU NEED:

VEGETABLE OIL
4 EGGS
8 SLICES BREAD
BUTTER
MAPLE SYRUP OR POWDERED SUGAR

WHAT YOU DO:

1. Pour a tablespoon of oil on the grill.

2. In a shallow bowl or empty pie tin, beat the eggs together.

3. When the oil is hot, dip a piece of bread in the eggs, coating both sides. Put the coated bread on the grill.

4. When the egg coating on the bottom is cooked, flip the bread over with a pancake turner. When both sides are cooked, serve your toast with butter and maple syrup or powdered sugar.

Creamy Dip in a Bread Bowl

Cook in a pot

WHAT YOU NEED:

1 LOAF ROUND BREAD
1 CUP SHREDDED CHEDDAR CHEESE
3/4 CUP CREAM CHEESE
1 1/2 CUPS SOUR CREAM
1/4 CUP CHOPPED GREEN ONION
1/2 CUP CANNED GREEN CHILES

RAW BROCCOLI, CARROTS, AND CAULIFLOWER FOR DIPPING

WHAT YOU DO:

1. Lay out a piece of foil that's twice as long as the bread. Place the bread in the center and scoop the soft bread out of the middle, leaving a shell to make a bread bowl. Leave a $1/2$ to 1-inch shell all the way around. Set the scooped-out bread aside.

2. Mix together the cheddar cheese, cream cheese, sour cream, onion, and chiles in a bowl. Pour the mixture into the hollowed-out bread bowl.

3. Bring the edges of the foil together on top of the bread. Wrap the bowl completely with aluminum foil, then cover it with one more layer of foil and place it into the pit.

4. Cook for about 45 minutes. It's done when the cheese inside is hot and melted. Unwrap the foil and eat the dip with the extra bread and veggies. Then you can eat the bowl!

🔥 🔪 Old-Fashioned Tinfoil Dinners

Cook on the coals

WHAT YOU NEED:

1 POUND GROUND BEEF
1 EGG
SALT AND PEPPER TO TASTE
1 LARGE ONION, PEELED
2 POTATOES, PEELED AND SLICED

WHAT YOU DO:

1. Put the ground beef, egg, salt, and pepper into a 1-quart, sealable plastic bag. Seal and squeeze together until mixed. Set aside.

2. Slice the onion and peel and slice the potatoes.

3. Divide the meat mixture into fourths and form into patties.

4. On a sheet of heavy-duty tinfoil, place one meat patty, some onions, and some potatoes. Sprinkle with more salt and pepper if desired. Repeat to make three more dinners.

5. Fold tinfoil around each dinner to make a secure pouch. Wrap in a second layer of foil.

6. Place foil dinners in coals and cook approximately 30 minutes, or until the meat is cooked through and potatoes are soft. Check at 15 minutes.

Be careful when opening the foil pouches that you don't get burned from the steam!

🔥 Hawaiian Dinners

Cook on the coals

WHAT YOU NEED:

HAM LUNCH MEAT
PINEAPPLE CHUNKS
MANDARIN ORANGE SLICES
TERIYAKI SAUCE

WHAT YOU DO:

1. Chop lunch meat into chunks. Place about ½ cup lunch meat into the center of an aluminum foil square. Add a few pineapple chunks and oranges slices. Drizzle with teriyaki sauce.

2. Repeat to make a total of 4 dinners.

3. Wrap the dinners tightly in foil, and then wrap each with an extra piece of foil.

4. Carefully place the dinners on the coals and cook for about 15 to 20 minutes. Dinners are done when they are piping hot. Eat out of the pouch or over cooked white rice.

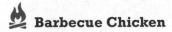 Barbecue Chicken

Cook on the coals

WHAT YOU NEED:

4 CHICKEN BREASTS
BARBECUE SAUCE
ALUMINUM FOIL
NEWSPAPER

WHAT YOU DO:

1. Lay out 4 sections of foil and place a chicken breast on top of each one.

2. Pour barbecue sauce over the chicken and then wrap the foil around it.

3. Lay out several sheets of newspaper and wrap them around the foil-covered chicken. Then cover with another layer of foil. Repeat.

4. Place the foil pouches in the coals and let the chicken cook for about 1 hour. Check at 30 minutes. The chicken is done when it is no longer pink in the center.

 **Hearty Chili**

Cook in a can—in the fire, on the stove, or on the grill

WHAT YOU NEED:

1 TABLESPOON BUTTER

1 CUP MEAT (GROUND SAUSAGE, GROUND BEEF, OR PEPPERONI CHUNKS)

1 CUP SLICED MUSHROOMS, GREEN PEPPER, ONION, OR COMBINATION

1 CAN (15 OUNCES) TOMATO SAUCE

1 CAN (15 OUNCES) STEWED TOMATOES

*1 TO 2 CUPS BEEF BROTH, VEGETABLE BROTH,
   OR WATER
SHREDDED MOZZARELLA OR CHEDDAR CHEESE
GOLDFISH CRACKERS (OPTIONAL)*

WHAT YOU DO:

1. Preheat a large, clean can by placing it in or over the fire. Wear oven mitts and use tongs when handling the hot can.

2. Melt the butter in the can. If using sausage or ground beef, add it to the butter and stir with a wooden spoon until it is nicely browned.

3. Add the vegetables and stir until cooked well (about 3 minutes).

4. Add the tomato sauce, tomatoes, and broth. If using pepperoni, add it to the mixture.

5. Cover your chili with aluminum foil and stir occasionally. Cook until warmed through, about 5 minutes.

6. Top with cheese and goldfish crackers, if using, or serve with a grilled cheese sandwich.

 Veggie Pie

Cook in a solar oven

WHAT YOU NEED:

2 CUPS COOKED, MIXED VEGETABLES (SUCH AS
    CARROTS, PEAS, AND POTATOES)
1 CAN CONDENSED CREAM OF MUSHROOM SOUP
1 CUP BISCUIT MIX
½ CUP MILK
1 EGG

WHAT YOU DO:

1. Mix the vegetables together with the condensed soup in a clean pie pan.

2. In a bowl, mix the biscuit mix, milk, and egg together. Pour the biscuit mixture on top of the veggies.

3. Place in the oven and cook about 45 minutes, or until the top is golden brown.

🔥 🔪 Moose Kabobs

Cook on a stick

WHAT YOU NEED:

1 POUND BEEFSTEAK
4 CUPS CUT VEGETABLES (CHOOSE FROM ONIONS,
BELL PEPPERS, ZUCCHINI, MUSHROOMS, AND
CHERRY TOMATOES)

*I CUP FRENCH, RUSSIAN, OR ITALIAN SALAD
    DRESSING*

WHAT YOU DO:

1. Cut steak and vegetables into 1-inch
   chunks. Ask an adult to help you with
   this.

2. Put meat and vegetables into a
   1-quart, sealable plastic bag. Add
   dressing.

3. Seal the bag and keep in the refrigera-
   tor or ice chest until time to use.

4. Skewer the meat and vegetables onto
   smooth sticks. You can use thin green
   twigs or branches you've collected, or
   buy wooden kabob skewers at the grocery store.

5. Cook over hot coals. Turn every 3 to
   4 minutes and cook until all sides are
   done (about 10 minutes).

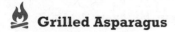 **Grilled Asparagus**

Cook on a grill

WHAT YOU NEED:

*1 BUNCH ASPARAGUS
1/4 CUP FRESH DILL OR 1 TEASPOON DRIED DILL
JUICE OF 1/2 LEMON*

WHAT YOU DO:

1. Chop an inch off the base of each asparagus spear. Throw away the chopped off parts.

2. Spread out a layer of aluminum foil that's 4 inches longer than the asparagus.

3. Place the asparagus on the foil. Sprinkle dill on top and then squeeze the lemon over everything.

4. Lay another sheet of foil on top of the asparagus and roll the ends of the foil

sheets together so the packet is completely sealed.

5. Place on a grill and cook for about 20 minutes, or until tender.

♨ Stuffed Mushrooms

Cook in a Dutch oven or on the stove, then on a stick

WHAT YOU NEED:

1/2 POUND GROUND BEEF
2 TABLESPOONS BUTTER
1/2 CUP BREADCRUMBS
1 CUP SHREDDED CHEDDAR CHEESE
8 LARGE FRESH MUSHROOMS
WOODEN OR METAL SKEWERS

WHAT YOU DO:

1. In a Dutch oven or on a stove, cook the beef until it is browned.

2. Add the butter, breadcrumbs, and cheese. Mix well.

3. Brush the mushrooms free of dirt and remove the stems.

4. Thread one mushroom cap onto a skewer, with the open part facing in.

5. Spoon some of the meat mixture into the mushroom.

6. Thread a second mushroom cap onto the skewer, with the open part facing the first one. This should enclose the meat mixture.

7. Repeat with the remaining mushrooms, using more skewers if needed.

8. Balance skewers across the fire. Turn occasionally and cook until warm.

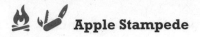 **Apple Stampede**

Cook in a can

WHAT YOU NEED:

4 TO 6 MEDIUM APPLES
1/2 CUP WATER
1/3 CUP SUGAR
2 TEASPOONS CINNAMON

WHAT YOU DO:

1. With an adult helper, peel, core, and cut apples into quarters.

2. Combine apples, water, and sugar in a clean, empty coffee can.

3. Cover with aluminum foil and cook over the coals about 20 minutes, until the apples are soft.

4. With an oven mitt, remove the can from the heat. Mash with a potato masher, fork, or clean rock.

5. Add cinnamon. Serve warm or cold.

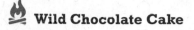 Wild Chocolate Cake

Cook in a pit

WHAT YOU NEED:

*1 LARGE PACKAGE CHOCOLATE PUDDING MIX
  (COOKED NOT INSTANT)
1 ⅔ CUPS MILK
1 PACKAGE CHOCOLATE CAKE MIX
2 EGGS
⅓ CUP VEGETABLE OIL
2 CUPS CHOCOLATE CHIPS*

WHAT YOU DO:

1. Line a Dutch oven with tinfoil.

2. In a pot or clean, empty coffee can,
   combine pudding mix and milk. Stir
   gently over heat until thick.

3. Remove from heat and stir in cake
   mix, eggs, and vegetable oil. Pour into

Dutch oven. Sprinkle chocolate chips on top and put on lid.

4. Lower the Dutch oven into the pit and cover with foil and dirt. Cook for about 1 hour.

Try this: Experiment with different flavor combinations. Try vanilla pudding and vanilla cake mix with butterscotch chips on top. Or try chocolate pudding and chocolate cake mix with peanut butter chips.

Orange Cakes

Cook on the coals or on the grill

WHAT YOU NEED:

6 LARGE ORANGES
1 BOX (8 OUNCES) JIFFY YELLOW CAKE MIX
INGREDIENTS ON BOX

WHAT YOU DO:

1. Slice the tops off the oranges. Remove the orange from the shell, being

careful not to damage the shell. You can eat the orange!

2. Prepare cake mix according to instructions. Fill each orange shell a little more than half full with cake mix. Replace top and wrap in foil.

3. Carefully place wrapped oranges on the coals or on a grill and bake about 30 minutes, turning often. When the cake is done, eat it out of the shell with a spoon.

Oatmeal Snacks

Cook in a solar oven

WHAT YOU NEED.

3 CUPS QUICK-COOKING OATS
1 CAN (14 OUNCES) SWEETENED CONDENSED MILK
1 CUP CHOCOLATE OR PEANUT BUTTER CHIPS
1 CUP DRIED CRANBERRIES OR RAISINS
1 CUP PEANUTS OR ALMONDS
3 TABLESPOONS BUTTER

WHAT YOU DO:

1. Mix all the ingredients except butter together in a large bowl.

2. Using 1 tablespoon of the butter, grease the insides of a muffin tin.

3. Melt the remaining butter in a pie tin or small can and stir into the oat mixture.

4. Press some of the mixture into each of the muffin cups.

5. Put the muffin tin in your solar oven and bake for 30 minutes. Let cool before serving.

 S'mores

Cook on a stick

WHAT YOU NEED:

GRAHAM CRACKERS
CHOCOLATE BARS
MARSHMALLOWS

WHAT YOU DO:

1. Break a graham cracker piece into a square and place a square of chocolate on top.

2. Roast a marshmallow until it is toasty brown.

3. Put the marshmallow on top of the chocolate square, then top with another square of graham cracker. Eat while it is warm and gooey!

Try this: Make your s'more more fancy by adding sliced fresh strawberry or banana. Or replace the chocolate with an Andes mint or caramel square. Experiment and have fun!

Metric Conversion Chart

Volume Measurements

U.S.	Metric
1 teaspoon	5 ml
1 tablespoon	15 ml
$1/4$ cup	60 ml
$1/3$ cup	75 ml
$1/2$ cup	125 ml
$2/3$ cup	150 ml
$3/4$ cup	175 ml
1 cup	250 ml

Weight Measurements

U.S.	Metric
$1/2$ ounce	15 g
1 ounce	30 g
3 ounces	90 g
4 ounces	115 g
8 ounces	225 g
12 ounces	350 g
1 pound	450 g
$2 1/4$ pounds	1 kg

Temperature Conversion

Fahrenheit	Celsius
250	120
300	150
325	160
350	180
375	190
400	200
425	220
450	230

SHOPPING LIST

CHAPTER FIVE

Outdoor Activities

THINGS TO DO

Most people camp to be close to nature. You'll enjoy your camping experience most if you use your senses: sight, hearing, touch, smell (but not taste!). Record your findings in a notebook. Don't worry about being a great writer or artist—just capture the memory. After several camping trips, you'll start to piece together the magic of how nature works.

Check out the birds, animals, and insects. What did they leave behind? Do you see animal tracks? Can you tell if the animal that made them was running, walking, or hopping? If you can't figure out who left them, you can look it up when you get home. Don't forget to look for teeth marks, too. Animals gnaw on tree bark, nutshells, pinecones, and leaves. Sketch anything unique: hollow trees, rabbit holes, spider webs, and scratches on tree trunks you find.

What do you feel when you are out-of-doors? Take off your shoes and squish the mud between your toes. Feel the bark of different trees. Are they rough or smooth? Cool or warm? Do some have moss on them? How does that feel? Is it dry or moist? Does it grow all around the tree or just on one side? Look at the other trees in the area. Is the moss growing on the same side? Why? Catch a salamander. Hold it for a moment. Is its slippery skin warm or cool? Put on your detective hat and see what you can discover. Ask questions. Find answers.

HIKING

A major activity when you go camping is hiking. Whether you set out on a short hike or an all-day one, hiking takes more effort than walking. Most people are in physical shape for hiking short distances. But stronger legs are needed for walking up and down hills, and stronger arms and shoulders for carrying a pack loaded with gear.

For those longer hikes, you may want to shape up a bit. Any physical activity you do beyond what you usually do will condition your body.

Here are a few stretches to limber you up. Do them before and after your other physical activities.

Peeping Owl

Plant your feet shoulder-width apart and bend your knees. Turn your head slowly to the right and try to peer over your right shoulder. Next, turn your head slowly to the left and peek over your left shoulder. Do this five times, s-l-o-w-l-y.

Rubber Wings

Place your feet shoulder-width apart and bend your knees slightly. Reach behind your head and put one hand between your shoulder blades. With the other hand, pull your elbow back. Hold that position for fifteen seconds. Do the same thing with the other arm.

Crumpled Crane

Sit on the floor with one leg straight out in front of you, your toes pointing up. Bend the other leg and put that foot against the straight knee (your bent knee will rest on the floor). Lean forward, reaching for your toes with both hands. Hold for fifteen seconds. Repeat with the other leg straight. Do this five times.

Grounded Butterfly

While sitting, put the soles of your feet together and clasp your ankles. Pull them toward you while your elbows rest on your knees. Hold for fifteen seconds.

Boulder Roll

Stand facing a wall with one foot ahead of the other. Place your hands against the wall at shoulder height. Bend the front knee and keep the back knee straight. Lean forward until you feel the stretch in your back leg. Hold fifteen seconds. Don't bounce. Repeat with the other foot forward. Do both five times.

FOOTWEAR

If your feet aren't happy when you hike, the trail will be a miserable place. A hiker with sore feet whines and limps and slows the hike to a stop.

The most important essential for happy feet is comfortable shoes or hiking boots that support your feet and ankles. You must be able to walk all day without rubbing blisters on your feet. Hiking boots are the best footwear for the trail. However, kids have growing feet and hiking boots are expensive. If your everyday athletic shoes fit well and are sturdy, they should work for most hiking.

If you'll hike often or in rugged or rocky terrain, hiking boots could prove a sound investment. When you buy hiking boots, go to a reputable outdoor shop. Ask questions and try on many pairs to find the right ones for you.

GAMES

Camping and games go together just like a picnic and ants! With no televisions, computers, or cell phones to distract you, and no schedule to keep, you'll have plenty of time to relax and enjoy playing. Generations of campers have made up games with just the materials they could find in their campground. Start by making a woods version of your favorite game.

Ball Games

For baseball, pitch a pinecone, dried seedpod, or whatever else is available to the batter, who will swing at it with a stick. Pinecones and seedpods can also become footballs. To play golf, use a stick club and pinecone or small stone ball. Use a cup or can on its side for the "hole" you hit the "ball" into.

Board Games

Play a game of checkers by drawing a
checkerboard in the sand and using
two colors of seashells or small stones
for checkers. And for tic-tac-toe, make
a grid in the dirt just like for checkers.
Use rocks for Xs and pinecones for Os,
or mark them in the dirt with your stick.

More Games

Try these other games and you'll know why campers through the ages have played them:

Don't Fall in the Ocean

1 or more players

Pretend all the land is the ocean. Rocks and logs are islands. Hop from one island to another. See how far you can go before you get wet. Playing this game will improve your balance—a skill you'll use often in the woods.

Cup Toss

1 or more players

Using a stick, draw a line you will stand behind in the dirt. Take four giant steps forward and set several drinking cups in a line. Left to right, give each cup a

number. If you have 4 cups, number them
1, 2, 3, and 4.

Stand behind your first line and toss
small stones or pinecones into the cups.
If you get the object in a cup, add the
number of that cup to your score. The
first player to reach 20 points wins.

Jump the Creek

1 or more players

Place two small sticks about 2 feet apart.
Pretend the space between them is a creek.
Stand behind one stick and "jump the
creek." When all the players have jumped
the creek, move one stick a few inches farther away. Take turns jumping. All players must be able to jump the creek before
it is widened. When one player is unable
to make it across, the team must work
together to get that camper across. Team
members hold the player's hands and, as
he jumps, pull him toward the other side.

If there is a real creek where you are camping, **AND AN ADULT SAYS IT IS OKAY**, jump the real creek. On hot days, you won't mind if you don't make it across! But only jump creeks that are shallow, with slow moving water and level bottoms.

Leaf Boat Race

2 or more players

Each player chooses a leaf or a twig to serve as a boat. You can only use things you find on the ground—nothing that is growing and that you have to pick.

Determine a place on the creek bank that will mark the end of the race. It might be beside a big rock or where a tree branch hangs over the water. Go upstream. One player calls out "Ready, Set, Go!" On "Go!" all the players drop their boats into the stream and run to the finish line to see whose boat wins. Remember, you must have adult approval anytime you play in or near the water.

Flashlight Games

You don't have to end the fun just because the sun goes down—not if you have a flashlight.

Have you noticed the odd shadows your flashlight casts on trees and rocks at night? You can create these shadows in your tent, too, and make up stories to go with them. All you need is a bright flashlight and your hands. Set up the flashlight to shine on a tent wall. It needs to be as far away from the wall as you are tall. Put your hands between the wall and the light and make different shapes. Use your hands to make a duck, person, or dog. If there are two people or more, each can be one of the characters. Now make up a story using the characters.

CAMPFIRE STORIES AND SONGS

When the chores are done and darkness falls, the campfire becomes the center of attention. You can be sure it won't be long until someone starts singing. Any tune you like is good for camp singing. Folk songs, cowboy songs, sea chanteys, and spirituals have long been campfire favorites.

You may already know such songs as "This Old Man," "Waltzing Matilda," "Kum Ba Yah," and "A-Roving." You can find more in songbooks at the library or bookstore. Here are a few to get you started.

Underwear
(to the tune of "Over There")

Underwear, underwear,
Send a pair, send a pair, I can wear;
For I left mine lying,
outside a-drying,
And now I need them, they're not there.
Underwear, underwear,
Get a pair, get a pair, anywhere;
The whistle's blowing,
I must be going,
For I must get there,
if I have to get there bare.

Mary Had a Swarm of Bees
(to the tune of "Merrily We Roll Along")

Mary had a swarm of bees,
Swarm of bees, swarm of bees,
Mary had a swarm of bees,
And they to save their lives
Were forced to go where Mary went,
Mary went, Mary went,
Were forced to go where Mary went,
For Mary had the hives.

We May Not Be The Warmest Bunch
(to the tune of "Battle Hymn of the Republic")

We may not be the warmest bunch
That ever hit the pike;
We may not be as handsome
Nor as swell as you would like.
But when it comes to camping stuff,
You'll grant that we can hike
Better than any kids in town.

Glory, Glory, Hallelujah!
Glory, Glory, Hallelujah!

Glory, Glory, Hallelujah!
His truth is marching on.

We wear our silk pajamas
in the summer when it's hot;
We wear our flannel nighties
In the winter when it's not.
And ofttimes in the spring
And ofttimes in the fall
We jump right in between the sheets
With nothing on at all.

Glory, Glory, Hallelujah!
Glory, Glory, Hallelujah!
Glory, Glory, Hallelujah!
His truth is marching on.

ANIMAL VOICES

Every animal has a different voice. Can
you identify a few? Listen for frogs, coy-
otes, and owls. Their voices are easy to
identify. If you hear a bird, see if you can
spot it. Then you can match the sound to
the bird. You'll amaze your friends when
you can identify a bird after hearing its

call. And it's not just animals that make sounds. Listen to the babbling brook and the wind in the tree branches. Can you find the words to describe them in your notebook? If you have a tape recorder, record the sounds to enjoy them when you get home.

ANIMAL TRACKS

When hiking any trail, you'll probably wonder whose home you are tromping through. You may not see many animals at first. They are expert listeners and sniffers and make a hasty departure when they know others are coming their way. But you can still find out who lives there. Use your detective skills. Animals leave telltale signs and you can learn to read many of them.

A good place to find signs is along a riverbank or lakeshore. Most animals go there for water sometime during the day, usually at dawn and dusk. When they do, they usually leave something behind—tracks.

A deer's track is different from that of a squirrel, a beaver, or a bear. Get a field guide of animal tracks and compare the ones you see to the ones in the guide to find out who's been there. Some animals leave tail or wing prints, too. And most animals leave scat (poop).

What if you want to see the animal, not just the tracks? There are two ways:

1. Sit very still. Watch and wait. You'll be surprised how much you really do see.

2. Track the animal. Before you do, make very sure it's an animal you want to find. You'll be happier when you suddenly come upon a squirrel, rabbit, or fox than if you crest a hill and find yourself face-to-face with a skunk, porcupine, or hungry bear. Enjoy watching those animals from a safe distance.

Here's how you track animals:

1. Make as little sound as possible. Unfamiliar sounds frighten away animals. To walk silently on hard ground put your toes down first. On soft ground, heels go down first.

2. Walk into the wind so your scent will be carried away from the animal, not toward it. Unfamiliar scents frighten away animals.

3. Learn what animals eat. If the animal you want to see is a berry eater, don't look for it in the willows; if it eats fish, don't waste time looking for it on the side of a hill.

You'll find many other signs left by animals—nests, burrows and mounds, stripped pinecones, tree bark gnawed or peeled away, tree trunks felled by chewing, branches nibbled, grass flattened. Who or what do you think did these things? Why? How? You'll never get bored hiking. There are too many mysteries to solve.

SMELLS

The fresh scent of pine, the sweet smell of wildflowers, the fishy smell near the water, the moldy smell on decaying plants in the shaded wetlands. Smells are hard to record, but keep a list of the things that you can identify. They are all part of your experience. Wood smoke from a campfire in the fall may become your very favorite scent.

How big is that track? What is that bug carrying? What kind of fur is caught on that branch? Along the trail you're going to see things you want to know more about.

BIRDS IN THE WOODS

A bird is a bird is a bird, right? Wrong. Though all adult birds have feathers, there are birds that fly and birds that can't. Some birds sip nectar from flowers, others crush seeds for the food stored inside, and even more nab insects, catch fish, or consume carcasses of unfortunate animals. Some roost on tree branches, others in hollow trees, while several burrow in the ground. Hummingbirds are so small their babies could fit in a thimble. But an ostrich, at eight feet tall and over three hundred pounds, is big enough for a grown person to ride.

You can learn a lot by just looking at a particular bird. Sketch it in your hiking journal so you can identify it later. Be sure to note the size you think it is and the color of its plumage. Look at its beak. Did you know you can tell what type food it eats by the shape of its bill?

Seed-eating birds have short, thick bills good for spitting and crushing seed shells. Insect eaters have streamlined, pointed beaks for grabbing insects from tight places or nabbing them in flight. Meat-eating birds have strong, pointed, hooked beaks needed for tearing meat. Water-bottom feeders have wide, flat bills for scooping and extracting food from mud. Fishing birds have spear-shaped bills for snatching or impaling frogs and fish.

You can identify a lot about a bird's habitat by its feet as well. Perching feet are small and agile for holding onto branches. Wading feet are long and skinny to keep the bird from sinking in mud. Swimming feet are webbed for pushing against water like paddles. Clutching feet are powerful with sharp, curved talons for holding onto prey.

Set aside one hike to learn just about birds. Before you go, learn to identify the birds in your area by their call. Take plenty of paper and colored pencils. Draw all the birds you see in one hour. When you get home, use a bird guidebook to identify the birds you saw. Write down some interesting facts about each bird. Do they live in your area all year or do they leave during the winter or summer? How many eggs do they lay? What does their nest look like? Which ones are swimmers, perchers, predators? What type of bill do they have? What do they eat? Does the male or female sit on the nest? Who feeds the babies?

Put all your drawings and notes about birds together. On an extra sheet of paper, write a little about your hike. Write down all the things you want to remember. Tell who went with you, what day you went, where you went, and what you saw. On yet another sheet of paper, glue a picture that was taken of you or your group. Add a title like "My Bird Hike" or "On the Trail of Little Birdie Feet," your name, and date of the hike. Once you attach a colorful cover, draw a tree full of birds on bright construction paper and you have a wonderful keepsake of your hike.

PLANTS

Plants are important! Some campers think plants are the least interesting part of being outdoors. After all, they don't run or swim or chirp or growl. Plants just

STAY SAFE!

Many berries you find are poisonous. The same is true of mushrooms that may be deadly toadstools. The water may have nasty germs in it. The wild animals know which things are safe to eat, but you should stick to the safe bet: hot dogs, s'mores, and other foods you brought from home.

stand there waving in the breeze. But, what would your camping area look like without them? You'd sit in the broiling sun to eat lunch rather than in the shade. There'd be no animals to watch because there would be no nuts, cones, berries, or greens to draw them there. Rain would wash away the hillsides with no roots to hold the soil in place. And everything would be the color of the dirt.

Here are some rules to keep in mind for keeping plant life thriving around you when you are camping:

★ Pick only a few leaves or flowers if you need them for a project. The plant needs most of them to make food for itself and the creatures that live nearby. The plant also needs them to attract pollinators. Leave plants rooted in the ground so they can keep growing.

★ Ask permission before picking leaves or flowers. It's against the rules to pick any living thing in many wilderness areas.

★ Never eat anything you find growing along the trail. Unless you know exactly what you are eating, you could get pretty sick or even die! Many poisonous berries look a lot like the tasty ones.

★ Take time to enjoy the many varieties of plants around you—trees that lose their leaves and those that don't, plants that have flowers and those with cones, ferns that are found in

moist places, and mosses that grow
on rocks. What else can you find?

★ Study plants. They are more interesting if you know about them. Look for
something amazing about each one.

SKIPPING ROCKS

Check out all the rocks when you go
camping. They can be a towering perch
or even a mountain. They can be a spot to
sit while you dangle your tired feet in the
cool water. Smaller rocks can be stacked
to mark your trail. Rocks can make a

pleasing kersplash when you skip them over the water. And teeny, tiny rocks make up the sand you squish between your toes.

Rocks are not all the same. And they change. Big rocks become little rocks, little rocks become sand. They don't change enough in a day or a year or maybe even a lifetime for us to notice, but they change. They are worn down by wind and rain, broken apart by fire and ice, carved by rushing river waters and crashing ocean waves.

Don't expect to skip a rock the first time you try or maybe not even the second or twenty-second time. But, don't give up. Once you can make a rock skip one time, try for two, then three. Some people can make one rock skip more than twenty times before it sinks. To skip rocks, try the following:

1. Gather a handful of flat, round rocks about the size of a small pancake down to the size of a fifty-cent piece.

2. Hold one between your thumb and forefinger, with your index finger wrapped around the rock's edge.

3. With your palm up and the rock flat, swing your arm back and to the side.

4. Bring your arm forward quickly, flick your wrist, and allow the rock to spin off the end of your index finger. The rock should skim across the surface of the water, touching down, and skipping to the next spot on the water.

STARGAZING

One of the great things about camping is that you are away from city lights so the whole night sky lights up with stars above you. Before you go camping, you may want to find a guidebook on stargazing that you can take with you. Take a compass and, if you have access to one, a telescope. Have an adult help you. Learn the stories of the constellations and how to find the North Star, the Big

Dipper, the Little Dipper, Orion's Belt and the planets.

Keep an eye out for motion in the sky, too. Maybe it's an airplane, a bird, or a bat. Shooting stars streak across the sky, and sometimes you can even see satellites in space or the International Space Station in orbit. Stargazing is a great nighttime activity for camping.

WRITE DOWN THE NOTES FOR A GAME YOU INVENTED

WRITE THE LYRICS TO A CAMPFIRE SONG

WRITE YOUR OWN GHOST STORY TO TELL AROUND THE CAMPFIRE

CHAPTER SIX

Camp Crafts

THINGS TO MAKE

When you are camping with a lazy afternoon stretched out before you, it's a great time to pull out the scissors, glue, paint, needle and thread, and make something. Let the creativity flow. Be inspired by the beautiful surroundings and connect with nature.

MAKE A CAMP COOKING APRON

Cooking around the campfire is much easier if you have your items organized with a cooking apron. Use the pockets to hold wooden spoons, spice packets, or things you need to keep handy to make your meal.

WHAT YOU NEED:

- ☐ a pair of old jeans (they don't need to fit)
- ☐ scissors
- ☐ measuring tape
- ☐ needle and thread
- ☐ two old neckties or a belt

WHAT YOU DO:

1. Cut the legs off the jeans, about 2 inches below where the insides of the pockets end.

2. Ask an adult to turn the jeans inside out and help you sew across each cut-off leg. Sew through the zipper placket, stitching it closed. Turn the pants back outside out. They should look more like a bag now, with two large pouches plus pockets for keeping your cooking utensils handy.

3. Put a belt around your waist, insert it through the back belt loops of your apron, and then fasten the buckle. Or, tie one necktie to each side belt loop, pull the apron to you, and then tie the neckties behind your back.

CREATE A CAMPFIRE COOKING NOTEBOOK

Take a notebook with you to record your camp cooking adventure. Use a lined notebook you get from the grocery store,

a hardbound nature journal from a bookstore or the ranger station, or a hand-
made book you make yourself. You can
make your own notebook by stapling or
sewing pages of paper together and using
a thicker paper or cardstock for the cover.
Decorate your notebook with drawings or
stickers. Make rubbings of trees or leaves.
Draw a picture of the lake. Go wild!

Inside your notebook, you can use the
space to plan meals and make shopping
lists. Then write the date of your cookout,
what you cooked, and how it turned out.
What kind of fire did you cook over? How
long did it take to cook the cheesy potatoes? Don't forget that adding strawber-
ries to your s'mores made them an extra
sweet treat. Make notes for cooking next
time and about what your favorite dishes
were. Ask your campmates to write about
your cookout too.

BUILD A FAMILY BANNER

It's fun to stake out your camp area
with a family banner. Craft stores sell

poster board, rolls of paper, fabrics, and
sometimes premade pennants and ban-
ners ready for painting. You'll also find
the markers, paint, stickers, and sten-
cils to help you identify your camp or
picnic area. Paint your family's name or
crest, and announce your name or theme.
When your banner is done, tie it between
two trees or hang it on the edge of the
picnic table.

MAKE A SWEATSHIRT WOOD CARRIER

A wood carrier makes gathering kindling
and tinder for your fire a whole lot easier.
If you are allowed to collect wood at your
site, try this out.

WHAT YOU NEED:

☐ an old sweatshirt or long-sleeved shirt

WHAT YOU DO:

1. Spread your shirt on the ground, with
    the arms stretched out.

2. Place sticks of wood up and down (not across) the torso of the shirt.

3. When you have about two armfuls of wood laid on the shirt, pull the sleeves in tightly and tie a knot. The shirt should hug the wood.

4. Hoist your bundle onto your back, using the sleeves to hold on to. Or you can tie the shirt around your waist or shoulders.

Now your hands are free to pick up extra wood or litter on the way back to camp!

WHITTLE THE PERFECT COOKING STICK

Sticks were probably the first cooking tools. Imagine cave dwellers in prehistoric times roasting woolly mammoth steaks on sticks! People have cooked food over fires on the ends of sticks ever since.

The kind of cooking stick you need depends on what you want to make. A long, thin stick with a sharpened end is good for cooking a single hot dog or marshmallow. Several hot dogs or marshmallows, or a large piece of meat like a pork chop, can be stuck onto a forked stick. A variety of meats and vegetables can be put on a thin stick to make a kabob.

A cooking stick should be green (growing) wood. Green wood doesn't burn easily. Willow grows along many stream banks. It is a good choice, but any green, non-poisonous wood will work. After making sure that it is allowed by your camping area, cut your stick about 3 feet long.

It should be thick enough that it won't bend when you put your food on it. Ask an adult to help you whittle one end to a point using a sharp knife.

MAKE A COAT HANGER COOKING STICK

You can make some reusable cooking sticks from clean coat hangers; then you won't have to look for sticks each time. You'll need to ask an adult for help with this project.

1. Cut the bottom of a wire coat hanger in two.

2. Straighten the cut sides.

3. Twist the two sides together. A stick inserted through the hook may help you twist.

4. Stop twisting about four inches from the end.

5. Bend the two ends into a fork shape.

Beware! The handle of this cooking stick will get hot as you cook with it. Always use your oven mitt to hold it.

Wash your cooking stick with hot, soapy water after each use. If the coating on your stick ever begins to peel, sand it smooth with sandpaper.

MAKE A TOILET PAPER HOLDER

Seal a roll of toilet paper in a half-gallon self-sealing plastic bag. Cut a slit in the bottom of the bag and pull the loose end of the paper through it. Poke two holes, one on each side of the bag, and run a 36-inch piece of string through one hole, through the toilet paper tube, and out the other hole. Tie the ends in a knot.

Now this holder can be hung from a branch by your pit toilet or around your neck where it's easy to reach when you need it. Caution: don't walk with the holder around your neck. It could get caught on a branch and choke you.

(Besides, the other campers would get a good laugh at your expense.)

🔥 PREPARE WATERPROOF MATCHES

Explorers waterproofed their matches by dipping them in melted paraffin (wax). Waterproofed matches are good to have while camping and it's fun to make them.

Have an adult heat paraffin in an old can. When it is taken off the heat, drop your matches in, pull them out with tongs or a fork, and let them cool. Another option for making waterproof matches is to paint the wooden matches with fingernail polish.

MAKE A HANDHELD PLANETARIUM

Make your own starry night!

1. Find an empty tin can with the top removed. Be careful of any sharp edges.

2. Place the can upright on a sheet of paper and trace around the can bottom.

3. Choose your favorite constellation and draw its stars within the circle onto the paper.

4. Cut out the circle, put it on the can bottom, and secure it with tape.

5. Using the awl on your pocketknife or a nail, pierce holes at each star, through the paper and the can.

6. Put a flashlight in the open end of the can. Turn it on and shine it on your tent wall. There's your constellation— and much closer than the real one!

CREATE A HIKING JOURNAL

Hiking is a favorite camping activity. Once you've warmed up, geared up, wised up, packed up, and filled up you're finally

ready to take a hike. What will you see?
Whether you hike in the forest, the desert, or near a swamp, you're sure to see
many wonders of nature. Walk at a lei-
surely pace; don't rush. You'll soon fall
into a comfortable stride. Take in the
sights, sounds, and smells of the area.
At each place you hike, you will see different things.

Watch for bird nests, snakeskins, feathers, nursery logs, mushrooms, fish, and
animal tracks. Soon you'll realize that
much of the fun of hiking is in studying
nature and much of the fun of studying nature is in the detective work. Who
made these tracks? What kind of bird
dropped this feather? Every good detective takes notes.

How about making a hiking journal for
your trek? You can include notes on the
date of the hike, weather conditions,
where you are going, and diagram of the
landscape. Sketch the animal tracks you
see along the creek, add a feather you

found, draw the tadpole you saw in the big puddle. Maybe later you can find out how long it will be before the tadpole becomes a frog. You can also add photographs from your hike—like the chipmunk that chattered at you while you ate lunch, and one of your big brother when he fell in the creek.

A hiking journal can be as simple as a pocket-sized spiral notebook with a pencil attached to it by a cord. But if you cover it like you might cover a schoolbook, with paper cut from a brown paper bag,

you can decorate the outside of your journal with your favorite hiking memories.

1. Cut a piece of heavy brown paper bag or decorative paper six inches wider and six inches taller than your opened notebook.

2. Place opened notebook on the paper so there is about the same amount of paper showing on the top and bottom and on each side.

3. Mark the paper with a pencil along the top and bottom of the notebook.

4. Fold the top down and the bottom up along the lines you just marked. Your paper should now be the same height as your notebook.

5. Cut the last three inches of one side forward and insert the notebook cover into the flaps created at the top and bottom. Neatly fold and tape the cover flap to the cover at the top and bottom.

Do the same with the other side.

6. Decorate with markers, crayons, colored pencils, or watercolors. It's hard to decide on a design. You could draw a mountain, sunset, rainbow trout, or an odorific skunk chasing a bear. Can't decide? Make several.

MAKE A PERSONALIZED HIKING STICK

A hiking stick gives you something to lean on when the trail is steep or rocky, steadies you when you cross a stream, and provides something to hang onto at the end of the day when you are too pooped to go any farther.

1. Select a straight sturdy stick about shoulder height.

2. If you want, peel off the bark carefully with a pocketknife. Cut away from your body and be careful not to cut yourself or hit your knees with the knife.

3. Wrap the grip area with a soft leather strip to cushion your hand. Tuck ends under the wrapped strip.

4. Personalize your stick by adding designs with markers or paint. Or you can carve patterns into your stick. Be careful when handling your pocketknife.

To make your walking stick into a "hear stick," tie three or four loud bells onto a cord or leather boot string. Wrap that around the arm of the stick and tie securely.

CREATE A BUG CAMP

Sometimes it's great to study nature up close. With this bug camp, you can examine nonpoisonous creepy crawly friends and then set them free.

WHAT YOU NEED:

☐ Magnifying glass
☐ Ruler

- [ ] Tweezers
- [ ] Pocket-sized field guide
- [ ] Sketch pad/pencil/colored pencils
- [ ] Small plastic jar
- [ ] Small plastic magnifying glass
- [ ] Scissors
- [ ] Craft knife
- [ ] Hammer and nail
- [ ] White glue

WHAT YOU DO:

1. Cut a hole in the jar's lid slightly smaller than the magnifying glass. You may find it helpful to make a circle of holes first, using the hammer and nail, then cut between the nail holes with a craft knife to make the large hole. Ask your adult helper to assist with this.

A WORD ABOUT COLLECTING

In the past, when your parents were young, people hauled rocks, feathers, bird nests, and other things home and made collections. Today, we know that these things are all a part of the land and are more valuable where they are than in the bottom of your closet. Now, collecting is done more with pictures, drawings, and memories. Keep a photo album, sketchpad, scrapbook, and hiking journal as your collection. Stack them neatly on a shelf where you can find them.

2. Make five or six airholes in the lid or jar using the hammer and nail.

3. Glue the magnifying glass onto the lid so it covers the large hole.

4. Find an insect to study. Look under logs, rocks, or leaves. Avoid ticks, wasps, poisonous spiders, or other dangerous insects. Refer to your field guide. Be sure to set the bug free from the jar when you are finished looking at it. Don't keep it in bug camp more than a few hours.

CREATE NATURE RUBBINGS

Many people have done rubbings of leaves, but did you know you can make rubbings of other things as well? Want to remember the unusual tree bark? Do you really like the texture of a rock? Want to make a border of grass blades on a page of your journal to remember a special picnic spot? Make a rubbing.

WHAT YOU NEED:

☐ hiking journal or other paper
☐ pencil/crayon

WHAT YOU DO:

1. Lay one sheet of your open journal or other paper on the tree trunk or whatever texture that you want to make a rubbing of.

2. Using the side of your pencil or crayon, gently rub it back and forth on your paper over the texture you want to capture.

3. Try making a border of one texture around another texture. Use that special page for something you want to highlight—a poem about the place you made the rubbings, a photograph, or something important to you.

Use this same technique to make special note cards, wrapping paper, bookmarks, or anything else you can think of.

DRAW YOUR FAMILY CREST OR PATTERNS YOU COULD PUT ON A BANNER

MAKE A RUBBING OF SOMETHING YOU FOUND WHILE CAMPING